Herding dogs : progressive training /

636.7 HOL   23150

Holland, Vergil S.
Sheridan County Library

DATE DUE		
FEB 6 2001		
MAY 1 4 2003		
JUN 2 4 2004		
JUL 1 9 2011		
FEB 2 0 2013		
AUG 1 2 2015		
MAR 2 7 2018		
MAR 2 5 2020		
SEP 0 1 2022		

THE LIBRARY STORE   #47-0120

O9-CFS-990

HERDING
—DOGS—
Progressive Training

Vergil S. Holland

SHERIDAN COUNTY LIBRARY
100 West Laurel Avenue
Plentywood, Montana 59254
765-2310

HOWELL
BOOK HOUSE
New York

Copyright © 1994 by Vergil S. Holland

All rights reserved. No part of this book may be reproduced or transmitted in any form or by any means, electronic or mechanical, including photocopying, recording, or by any information storage and retrieval system, without permission in writing from the Publisher.

Macmillan General Reference
A Simon & Schuster Macmillan Company
1633 Broadway
New York, NY 10019-6785

MACMILLAN is a registered trademark of Macmillan, Inc.

Library of Congress Cataloging-in-Publication Data

Holland, Vergil S.
    Herding dogs: progressive training/by Vergil S. Holland.
        p.   cm.
    ISBN 0-87605-644-3
    1. Herding dogs—Training.   2. Livestock protection dogs—
Training.   I. Title.
SF428.6.H65   1994   9/00   23150
636.7'0886—dc20   Ingram   94–1542
  13.17/21.95   CIP

Manufactured in the United States of America
10 9 8 7

This book is dedicated to
Robin
a special dog, companion and friend.

Robin

Contents

Acknowledgments

THIS BOOK could not have been written without the constant help and encouragement of my wife, Bonnie Holland. I would like to take this opportunity to recognize her for her miles and hours of listening to me talking into the tape recorder, for all of her hard work, which allowed me time for this book, and for keeping my eyes focused on the important things in life.

I would like to express special thanks to:

Chalmers Means, Roger Millen and Susan de Carvalho for thoughtful and careful reading, editing and suggestions.

All the herding students and trainers who have supported this effort and encouraged the development of this book.

All the herding dogs that have special places in our hearts.

Vergil and Bonnie Holland and their dogs.

Foreword

IT HAS BEEN my privilege to know Vergil Holland for over twenty years. I have witnessed his remarkable growth in training and teaching techniques for herding dogs and handlers through these years.

As an experienced handler and trainer of Border Collies, I greatly respect his expertise in gentle and kind methods of training and teaching. I have long realized the need for a good, descriptive training book written by someone who trains and uses stock dogs.

Vergil has actively pursued this endeavor for many years and has learned his methods from training, using and competing with stock dogs, as well as by watching and applying techniques of other trainers and handlers whom he admired and imitated.

This book is a culmination of his experiences and techniques. I feel it is the most descriptive, practical and explicit book yet compiled. The diagrams are set up and explained clearly. The text provides novice and experienced trainers and handlers with exercises and techniques that are described in detail and which will accomplish the desired results when applied.

I deeply appreciate Vergil's approach to training and the concept of teamwork between the handler and animal that goes beyond the outdated training theories of "breaking" dogs using cruel methods of brute force or painful devices.

I believe that all owners of herding dogs will benefit from reading this book. I hope you will enjoy it and use it to your advantage in training.

Walt Jagger
Professional Stock Dog Trainer
Noted Handler and Winner of
    Numerous Stock Dog Championships

Preface

HERDING IS AN ACTIVITY that can provide you and your dog with many hours of useful work and enjoyment. You may be considering training a herding dog for farm or ranch work, or as a way to enjoy working at an activity for which your dog was originally bred. For those interested in competitions, there are organized Herding Trials for purebred and mixed-breed dogs.

In this book I will describe and discuss the herding training program I have used with hundreds of handlers and dogs in clinics, lessons and training sessions. Understanding your dog and that dog's reactions is the basis for this program. It is a progressive program to guide you from a dog's first exposure to stock through advanced training for farm or trial work. I will discuss different movements and exercises, the reasons why I do certain things in specific ways and special problems that may arise during each phase of training. I will also present principles of the instinctual basis for herding, and reactions of the dog to stock and to training.

Sections on herding commands and terms, basic obedience for the stock dog and working different types of stock (ducks, cattle and sheep) are included.

Special chapters on personality types of different stock dogs and training modifications that may be necessary for these personality types should enable you and your dog to progress toward achieving your maximum potential.

In many cases I use the Border Collie as the standard of excellence for a herding dog. This is because the Border Collie is one of the few breeds that has been bred *exclusively* for herding over hundreds of years. This emphasis on herding performance has resulted in preservation and perpetuation of the herding instinct and natural ability, as well as selection for the temperament that is easily trained for herding.

In this book I will also discuss specific characteristics and training techniques for Herding breeds other than Border Collies, based on my years of experience with a variety of breeds in clinics, lessons and training situations.

"Loyalty"

GOD SUMMONED a beast from the fields and He said, "Behold people created in my image. Therefore, adore them. You shall protect them in the wilderness, shepherd their flocks, watch over their children, accompany them wherever they may go—even into civilization. You shall be a companion, an ally, a slave.

"To do these things," God said, "I endow you with instincts uncommon to other beasts: faithfulness, devotion and understanding surpassing that of people. Lest it impair your courage, you shall never foresee your death. Lest it impair your loyalty, you shall be blind to the faults of people. Lest it impair your understanding, you are denied the power of words. Let no fault of language cleave an accord beyond that of people with any other beast—or even people with other people. Speak to your people only with your mind and through your honest eyes.

"Walk by their sides; sleep in their doorways; forage for them; ward off their enemies; carry their burdens; share their afflictions; love them and comfort them. And in return for this, people will fulfill your needs and wants—which shall be only food, shelter and affection.

"So be silent, and be a friend to people. Guide them along the way to this land that I have promised them. This shall be your destiny and your immortality." So spoke the Lord.

And the dog heard and was content.

Author Unknown

Natural ability, an extension of instinct, refers to the ability of the dog to read stock and situations and to react appropriately. This four-month-old Border Collie already shows a good deal of intensity and talent.

1

Introduction to the Training of Stock Dogs

"Every dog and handler has peak performance potential—you just need to know where they are coming from and meet them there."

Vergil Holland

OVERVIEW

A personal philosophy is required to train your dog with fairness and consistency. Development of your personal philosophy regarding learning and training is important in helping you to understand the training program, to make progress at a rate best suited to you and your dog and to enjoy the small steps that add up to large gains over time.

You as the handler will need to understand concepts basic to herding and the terminology that is used in herding to describe herding dogs and to communicate with people about herding.

Instinct and natural ability play a major role in your dog's responses to livestock and to training. The concepts of pressure and balance form the basis for working stock. Reading your dog and stock is an important skill in using training situations to achieve the desired results. The ability to recognize when your dog is uncomfortable and how to create situations in which he learns to be comfortable is the basis for training.

If you are interested in training your dog for herding, certain facilities, equipment, types of stock, handler responsibilities and knowledge about your dog's characteristics will make your job easier and more enjoyable. Careful consideration of all of these factors should enable you to get the most out of your training.

PHILOSOPHY OF TRAINING

My philosophy of training is built on four basic premises. They are progressive, dog-based and aimed at producing a well-rounded dog and at maximizing the potential of the individual dog and dog/handler teams:

1. **Progressive** You make progress by building on previously learned skills. You do not try difficult situations before you have mastered easier ones. During early stages of training, the natural instincts and abilities of the dog are used to establish certain reactions and associations. In later stages of training, progressive work continues by building on previously learned exercises and sequences of movements. Retention of instinct and natural ability in the dog is of the utmost importance throughout the training program.

2. **Dog-based** Each dog is an individual with unique developmental rates of progress and different strengths and weaknesses. Good training requires constant reading and understanding of the dog and aims to preserve a good attitude, on the part of dog and handler, at all times. The exercises to be mastered, as well as the order and pace at which they are approached, depend upon the response of the dog. This program allows dogs with weaknesses or difficulties in one area to progress more rapidly in other areas, and does not recommend repeated "drilling" in an area that has already been learned. The variety of exercises and flexibility of the program allow each dog and handler to succeed in mastering components at their own pace. This element of experiencing success is critical for continued enjoyment of herding for both the handler and the dog!

3. **Aimed at producing a well-rounded dog** Good herding training produces a well-rounded dog that can work in many practical, real-life situations, and that is useful either on the farm or in competition.

4. **Aimed at maximizing the potential of the individual dog and dog/handler teams** No "perfect" dogs or people exist. Herding requires a *true partnership* between the dog and handler. It provides the ultimate challenge to the handler to come up to the dog's level, to communicate in a complex and constantly changing environment. It provides the ultimate challenge to the dog as well, who must continually adjust to changes in the environment, sheep and handler commands. This requires that the dog use the instincts and natural abilities of his world, but also be able to move into our world in order to respond to the desires of the human partner. The ability to adjust to and accept constant movement between the dog's world and our world is truly a lot to ask of a dog, and it is this wondrous ability that provides much of the beauty and fascination of herding!

GENERAL PRINCIPLES OF HERDING

Instinct

Instinct is the basis from which all other herding principles and working terms are derived. Herding instinct refers to the desire of the dog to *do something* with the stock. There are many differences and variations in the ways this instinct is displayed; these differences distinguish among breeds of stock dogs and among individual dogs within each breed.

Generally, dogs can be categorized according to whether they are "gathering" or "driving" dogs. *Gathering dogs have the desire to group or round up the stock. Heeling or driving dogs have the desire to push or drive stock away from the handler, with little or no desire to collect or bring them back.* Therefore, dogs with an instinct to drive stock require a different training approach than dogs with an instinct to gather the stock. In some breeds, you may see varying degrees of one or both of these instincts.

Dogs with gathering instincts, when initially exposed to stock, may circle around the outside of the stock, bring the stock to the handler or try to hold the stock in one place against a fence. They usually watch and work on the heads of the stock. Heeling or driving dogs tend to fall in behind the stock as they move. The biggest difference between a gathering and driving dog is that the *gathering dog* will eventually work *on*, as well as *for*, the handler, while the *driving dog* will be working *for* the handler; it matters little to the driving dog whether he is moving the stock away from or toward you. The driving dog also may have the desire to ''head'' the stock and, if holding the stock against a fence, may appear much like a gathering dog, although there is a different purpose in mind. Both gathering and driving dogs often have the desire to hold stock motionless. Any time the stock start to move or run, these dogs will try to ''head'' or stop the stock.

Certain breeds characteristically tend to exhibit either gathering or driving instincts. Some breeds or individuals within a breed may not display a distinct preference for either driving or gathering. Border Collies are almost exclusively gathering dogs; many dogs of other herding breeds also are gathering dogs; however, generally speaking, Queensland Heelers, Australian Shepherds and Corgis have stronger driving/heeling tendencies.

The display of a particular type of instinct will affect the training program, but should not limit the dog to performing only this task. *Any trained stock dog, regardless of breed, should eventually be able both to gather and to drive stock.*

Natural Ability

Natural ability, an extension of instinct, refers to the ability of the dog to read stock and situations and to react appropriately. Natural ability may be the first trait to disappear when breeding programs start selecting for traits other than herding ability! Not all dogs with the instinct to herd will also have natural ability in herding. Dogs come with numerous and varying degrees of natural ability. *A dog with less natural ability may be more easily trained*, because the inbred desire to do what comes naturally is less intense. However, when the dog is later asked to work independently, he is likely to have more trouble because of his lesser degree of natural ability. This type of dog is easily made into what is termed a ''push-button dog,'' meaning one that works exclusively from the handler's signals rather than from the dog's own reading of situations.

A dog with a lot of natural ability may not be easy to train. However, in the end, this dog is more useful and well rounded. A high

This Border Collie puppy, at the age of four months, already shows the desire and the natural ability to gather the sheep. In some breeds or individual dogs, this sustained interest may not be evident until between the ages of ten and fourteen months.

level of natural ability seems to be the result of a combination of intelligence, good attitude, desire to herd and desire to please the handler, as well as the ability to read pressure and balance.

Pressure

Pressure is a force that is felt by the dog and is initially generated by the desires or movements of the stock. Later in training, the dog will feel pressure generated by both the stock and the handler. The dog's responses are governed by internal reactions to pressure. A different type of pressure also may be generated by the dog, i.e., putting pressure on the stock to move. Yet another type of pressure can be exerted by the handler on the dog—the pressure of excessive demands, often resulting in expecting and asking too much from a young dog too quickly.

These pressures generated by the stock, handler and environment may cause a young dog to feel the need to react constantly. This youngster may not always know *how* to react to the pressures being felt, and thus these reactions may take several forms, depending on the instincts and natural abilities of the dog. As a handler, it is your responsibility to try to understand these pressures the dog is feeling, and to help him learn the most desirable ways to react to them.

This ability to "feel" pressure is what makes a stock dog. A dog with an abundance of this ability to read what a sheep is thinking can, at first, be an almost insurmountable problem to the new handler. Different breeds have varying degrees of ability in this area. Because of years of careful selection, Border Collies generally have a highly refined ability to read the pressure, or the sheep's desire to move, even *prior* to actual movement.

Balance

Balance is the basis for the dog's ability to move the stock, regardless of the type of instinct that is present. This is the most important concept for the beginning handler to understand. Balance is based on movement by the sheep and the dog's reaction to this movement, so that the dog is placing himself properly in relation to the sheep and handler. From the dog's viewpoint, the "proper place" is the position that best prevents the escape of the sheep from the handler. The dog's instinctual goal is to "establish balance" or "reach a balance point" that results in stopping all movement of the stock.

Relationship of Pressure and Balance

The concepts of pressure and balance are intimately related and are based on actions of the sheep and/or handler and reactions by the dog:

1. *Movement* by the sheep (or handler) creates an *action*.
2. This action generates *pressure* to which the dog *reacts*.
3. The dog reacts in such a way as to establish or achieve *balance* (lack of movement by the sheep).
4. When all pressures are equalized, balance has been achieved or the dog has "reached the balance point." This is the point at which the dog feels the stock are most under control or least likely to escape. This equalization of pressures, creating balance, is the result of herding instinct and ability.

In the case of the *gathering dog*, pressures are equalized and balance is reached when sheep are brought and held to the handler,

6

Balance is based on movement by the sheep and the dog's reaction to this movement, so that the stock dog is placing himself at the proper place in relation to the sheep and handler. This puppy, long before the beginning of a training program, already shows the desire to reach the balance point by moving in a clockwise direction in relation to the handler.

As this magnetic board display demonstrates, balance and pressure are influenced by external factors such as gates or the presence of other sheep.

whether the handler is moving or standing still. With the *heeling or driving dog*, pressures are equalized and balance is reached when the sheep are either immobilized (as when against a fence) or moved off in any direction.

In the early stages of training it is extremely important to preserve natural instinct and ability by allowing the dog to reach the balance points. If you do not pay attention to and understand pressures and balance, you may create very stressful conditions. By repeatedly asking your dog to disregard the pressures or repeatedly asking him to stop when out of balance, you may be discouraging to the point that the dog "turns off" (no longer wants to work sheep). Or, it could undermine your dog's confidence and ability to work or read stock to the point that this ability is not expressed or even disappears! Young stock dogs must feel that they are "winning" with regard to balance (obeying "instinct over command") and must slowly be brought to understand that they do not always have to "win" (establishment of "command over instinct").

As you progress with your dog, you will both learn to work with balance and use it to your advantage. Changing and rechanging balance is required in order to apply the pressure needed to accomplish specific tasks. For example, in order for a gathering dog to drive sheep away from you, that dog must apply pressure from the rear, a circumstance that goes against the instinct to gather. To drive or pressure the sheep to move in a straight line, your dog cannot use the same pressures used when holding the sheep still. A dog must create an unequal but constant pressure in order to react to the wayward tendencies of the sheep while keeping the flock moving in the desired direction. This ability does not come easily for dogs with strong gathering instincts! But, because of the dog's respect for and desire to please you, he is able to learn to control his natural desires and use his instincts and abilities according to your directions.

The driving dog, because of his natural instinct to push or drive stock away, must be taught to gather the stock. Because of his natural instinct to drive, this may be difficult. But, because of the dog's desire to please the handler, the instinct to drive may be overcome and the dog taught to gather or fetch (bring the sheep to the handler).

Reading and Understanding Your Dog

Being able to read and understand your dog during training and throughout life is very important. It can make the difference between

8

your ending up with a good dog, a mediocre dog or a poor dog. The pressure from your demands is a much different type of pressure than that exerted by *movements* of the sheep or handler or by features of the environment. Inappropriate demands (not necessarily commands) cause undue pressure that may not be appropriate for an individual dog at a particular stage of maturity, development or training. Failure to recognize when demands are inappropriate or excessive for an individual dog can be very detrimental to your young dog!

As you start working, be attentive to your dog's attitude and actions. Signs of pressure from inappropriate demands may include seeing the dog repeatedly turning his head away from the sheep, loss of interest or enthusiasm or a drop in overall countenance. In extreme cases, the dog may end up leaving the field.

If you see any of these symptoms, immediately re-evaluate your procedures. Analyze whether principles of balance and pressure are being violated. *Lighten up immediately!* Change your routine or go to a different phase of work. Remember, you are not in a race. You won't receive a special prize for the fastest-trained dog, but you can enjoy many satisfying years of herding with the best-trained dog!

Understand that the dog wants desperately to do what you want. But, at the same time, your dog feels a need to do what he's been bred to do—follow his instincts. It is important that you take control and slowly strengthen the dog's desire to please over the impulse of natural instincts, as you gradually establish command over instinct. *Any time you force command over instinct without the dog being willing to give, you may leave "holes" in both mental attitude and general work.* These holes may or may not be mended throughout a dog's career. The goal is to end up with a highly trained animal without losing any of the valuable natural ability with which you started! That's why I stress the need to be constantly reading your dog for stress-related problems during your training program.

To me the challenge of training a herding dog without loss of natural ability is one of the most exciting parts of developing a well-trained dog. When you are working and giving commands one right after another, the properly trained dog is reacting in this way: The dog hears your command and reacts instantly, then goes back to his own thinking pattern. The dog hears another command, reacts to adjust to the handler and is instantly back to his own instincts to read the pressure and balance according to that latest command.

Another way to look at this is envisioning the handler as the "coach" and the dog as the "player." You send in the signal and immediately the dog responds. At the same time, your dog must independently think how best to carry out the command, relying on natural ability. This makes an almost unbelievable task that these dogs must do! They must instantly react to a signal and then re-enter their instinctive world to react to the changes in pressure in order to fulfill your last command. Is it any wonder that so many dogs get ruined or set back in the early stages of training? Be careful! *Read your dog constantly!*

Reading Your Sheep

Being able to read your sheep is important for you to help your dog, but it is not always easy. Reading your sheep means that you should pick up signals about what the sheep are going to do before they actually do it. This can be very difficult, especially if you are not used to working with stock. Overall, it's the basic component of getting the job done—on or off the trial field. Once your dog is trained, reading sheep can become both an art and a science.

From the start of your training program, practice reading your sheep. If they moved when you didn't expect them to, ask yourself, Why did that occur? What signals did I miss? Try to figure it out. Consider different things the sheep might do and decide what you may be able to do to prevent them from deviating from the path you would like them to follow. There is only so much a teacher can teach on this subject. A big part of it is working with stock and being around them until reacting to their movements is almost involuntary. You must watch for little clues like the turning of the head (which may indicate possible direction of movement), movement of the ears (indicating alarm), the position of the head: If the head is high they may be ready to run; if the head is low the sheep may be feeling sullen or stubborn. You also need to remain tuned in to the feelings of your dog. Remember, the dog knew how to "read" sheep long before you did!

Your Dog's Comfort or Discomfort

Much of the training will depend on understanding when your dog is comfortable or uncomfortable. It is a challenge in training to help a young dog realize when he is comfortable and to prevent him from becoming uncomfortable.

For example, when you are in a situation in which you are not in control, you are probably uncomfortable. When you feel in control,

10

you feel at ease or comfortable. Your dog has these same basic feelings, and certain situations will cause comfortable or uncomfortable feelings.

A situation that typically results in discomfort for the dog is working too close to the sheep. To illustrate this concept, think of your cat out on the lawn watching a bird. The cat starts out at a distance from the bird, and although intent on the bird, the cat is fairly relaxed (and comfortable). As a cat moves toward the bird, that cat's body language changes—it becomes very intense, as the cat crouches, muscles rippling and tail starting to switch. The closer the cat gets, the more intense it becomes. When just ready to spring, the cat is extremely uncomfortable. At a critical point in approaching the bird, the cat's "kill mechanism" is triggered as it springs. This is nature's way of making sure that the cat gets fed. The same forces are at work with regard to your dog's distance from the sheep.

The dog's being too close makes the sheep edgy and causes them to speed up. When the sheep get edgy, the dog senses it, fears a loss of control and begins to feel uncomfortable. He speeds up a little not knowing what else to do and is relying on instincts. As the dog comes in closer and closer, the "kill mechanism" is triggered, often resulting in a grip (bite). This is why all trainers and teachers will emphasize getting the dog "off" or "away from the sheep."

By forcing the dog to stay back, you will help your dog stay comfortable. When a dog is farther back, the sheep relax and the dog can relax and feel in control of the situation. By feeling in control, the dog feels comfortable. This causes things to go smoothly and gives you and your dog time to think. If you are careful to keep the correct distance from the sheep, your dog will soon learn how to create this comfortable situation independently. Maintaining a distance from the sheep that enables the dog to be comfortable is referred to as maintaining a "comfort zone." The distance necessary to establish and maintain a comfort zone will vary with different dogs, stock and situations.

Another situation in your training that can cause discomfort is forcing a young dog to stop off balance to you and the sheep. This goes directly against the dog's instincts and creates a form of stress that can be very detrimental for the dog in the beginning stages of work. I am not sure which causes the most stress to an animal with a lot of natural ability—the force it takes for you to stop the dog off balance, or the actual stopping off balance. I do know it can cause many problems! The dog may lose enthusiasm, tend to become a "push-button dog" (who responds only to commands), learn to distrust

The picture above shows a Belgian Tervuren in an uncomfortable position, too close to the sheep, which may cause the dog to grip. In the picture below, the German Shepherd is wearing at the proper distance from the sheep, and both dog and sheep are relaxed. Maintenance of a distance between the sheep and dog that enables the dog to be comfortable is referred to as maintaining a "comfort zone."

the handler or establish the habit of disobeying. In extreme cases, the dog may leave the field or just quit wanting to work stock.

As Mari Jones, farm dog expert and author, has written, ''A dog's aim should be to win the confidence of the sheep and ensure their cooperation. He should be able to come right up to them and even come among them, scattering them in all directions. The secret is to master them without agitating them, to create a kind of kinship with them by making them feel that he knows what he is trying to do, without bumbling about in uncertainty or rushing around unnecessarily. A good dog realizes that there is purpose in his every movement. Under the guidance of his master's voice, he knows that he will be moving to a pattern as his master tells him each movement in turn. No, he does not know the pattern, but he does know obedience—the obedience which comes from trust in his master.'' So, as you use this training program, remember that your goal is to create a comfortable situation or environment for the young dog, to help the started dog to understand what is wanted and feel comfortable in a variety of situations.

PREPARING TO TRAIN YOUR STOCK DOG

Facilities

To train a stock dog, the handler should possess or have access to certain basic facilities, intended for the safety of the dog, the stock and the handler. Such facilities include a fairly level field of at least 150 yards by 125 yards. This field ideally should be fenced with woven wire of sufficient height (at least 36 inches) to discourage sheep from jumping out of the field and to prevent escape of the sheep should they bolt. Just as important as keeping stock *in* is the capacity to keep predators and roaming dogs *out*. Fencing should be kept in good repair and as safe as possible in order to prevent the stock or dog from being injured and/or entangled.

A round or oval pen (approximately 75 feet by 100 feet) constructed of fencing capable of taking abuse and preventing injury should be used for the initial introduction to livestock, especially if starting a breed other than a Border Collie. Such a pen is useful in starting a Border Collie also, particularly if you are inexperienced or do not have a friend with an experienced dog to help move and hold the sheep in position.

Chutes and small pens will be helpful for stock management as well as for teaching your dog to work comfortably in close-contact situations.

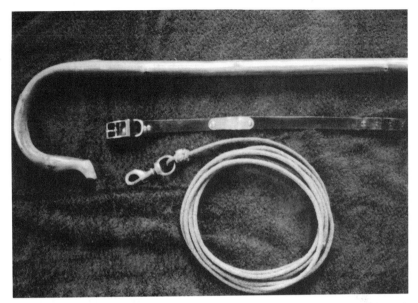

Necessary equipment includes a flat buckle collar for the dog, a long line and a crook. A "Boogie Bag" can be constructed by taping a rolled-up dog food bag (50 lb. sack) or plastic bag to a 2- to 3-foot piece of PVC conduit or a shortened crook. The crook should extend into the bag for 1 to 1½ feet (see below).

15

Using an oval ring helps keep the sheep and dog under control during the initial training, when chasing stock "all over the field" can become a disaster! Sometimes it is slightly more difficult to keep the stock off of the fence and in the middle of the small ring, but usually it is worth this inconvenience to have the control that the small space provides. Although the time spent working in the small oval ring will be relatively short, it is handy to be able to go back to the small ring to correct certain problems or to teach certain exercises.

A pen with a gate set into the fence, and a movable pen made of panels, will be needed for the stages of training that involve penning. International Border Collie rules state that the pen should be 2 meters by 3 meters (slightly less than 6 feet by 9 feet) with the gate on the 2 meter side; any size pen down to 5 feet by 5 feet will be suitable for training.

An enclosure or fenced alleyway of approximately 16 feet by 20 feet will be needed for close contact work, and to teach your dog the "Go Back" command.

Access to a shed, barn or shelter is useful for managing stock that may become sick or injured and for providing shelter during cold or wet weather.

Equipment

Necessary equipment includes a flat buckle collar for the dog, a long line and a crook. The flat buckle collar should fit snugly; it should not pull off over the dog's head. The long line should be 15 to 20 feet in length, made of 3/16- to 5/16-inch woven cord with a small bolt snap. The line and snap should be light so that the dog will scarcely know the line is present. The line is meant to be a convenience and training aid for the handler. The crook may be made of plastic (½-inch PVC electrical conduit) or of wood, and should be approximately 5 feet long.

A "boogie bag" may be useful in some stages of training. This tool can be constructed by taping a rolled-up dog food bag (50-pound sack) or plastic bag to a 2- to 3-foot piece of PVC conduit or a broken crook. The crook should extend into the bag for 1 to 1½ feet. The boogie bag is useful for projecting a lot of force when it is slapped on the ground, and will not hurt the dog if it does connect with him.

I have never found special training collars or long PVC poles to be necessary, but they may be useful with certain dogs or handlers.

16

Sheep are ideal for beginning to train a stock dog because of their instinctive desire to group together.

Stock

Dogs may be trained to herd a variety of types of stock. I prefer to use sheep for training dogs because of the sheep's instinctive desire to group together. Dorset crosses, since they are very even-tempered and steady, are a good breed for starting dogs. Black-faced sheep, such as Suffolks, may be more flighty and temperamental and less apt to stay in a group. Although dogs will need to learn to work all types and breeds of sheep during their training, the sheep used in the initial sessions should be easily controlled and not aggressive. That is, they must be "dog-broke." This means that they are used to being worked by a trained stock dog and are not afraid of people. Dog-broke sheep should easily move away from a dog and go to the handler.

For the novice handler of any breed, or when starting any breed other than a Border Collie, the type of dog-broke sheep I recommend are those that I call "knee-knockers." These sheep are trained to go to the handler's knees and stay with the handler. They will not charge past the handler or drift away. Knee-knocker sheep also are recommended when working with any dog that is very one-sided and grips (bites) when going in the uncomfortable direction.

Starting dogs on sheep that are not dog-broke and not accustomed to people can result in severe frustration and can cause problems that may take weeks or months to correct. Dog-broke and knee-knocker sheep may be available from professional herding trainers or experienced herding enthusiasts in your area. It is worth the trouble and expense to start out with these kinds of sheep!

A minimum of five to ten sheep is recommended, but a flock of at least ten to thirty sheep is preferred. This allows variation in number and type of sheep that may be of benefit in working with your dog. Some exercises are more easily done and some problems are more easily addressed when using at least twenty sheep.

Handler Attributes

Handlers of all ages and types can be successful at herding. However, during the early stages of training there may be certain physical demands associated with training an inexperienced dog—the sheep may bump you, walk on your feet or mill around you, causing you to lose your footing. Even the most experienced handlers will occasionally meet the ground when working with an inexperienced dog. If things get a little too wild, the sheep may charge toward you with considerable momentum, necessitating quick reactions or movement on your part to prevent a crash.

Depending on the reactions of the dog, training may require the handler to move swiftly, running around or through the sheep, in order to teach the dog what is expected.

If you are unsure about whether you are physically capable of undertaking herding, evaluation by an experienced herding trainer is recommended. It may be beneficial to have a professional train your dog during certain stages if you feel you are not agile enough to handle that particular stage or problem.

Once a dog is past the beginning stages, handling becomes less physically demanding. Many senior citizens very successfully handle dogs that have had some initial training. If you are physically fit and familiar with livestock, the physical demands should not be too great.

In addition to physical requirements, herding requires the handler's commitment to trying to understand or "read" the environment, the stock and especially the dog. The ability to read the environment, stock and dog is a constant challenge, even for experienced handlers, and provides the stimulation and exercise that appeal to those who enjoy mental challenges.

It requires commitment to provide consistent work, regardless of the weather, in order to make progress. Short training sessions (averaging fifteen to twenty minutes) at least three times per week are recommended in order to achieve any progress in herding training. Training sessions once a day, four to five times per week or more, are preferred.

Dog

You cannot force a dog to herd. The dog must have some degree of herding instinct in order to provide the interest necessary to work stock. Possession of instinct does not guarantee talent or ability in herding; but some lack of talent or ability can be offset through training and obedience.

At first, the young herding dog will work entirely on instinct and natural ability, a condition known as "instinct over command" (sometimes in spite of command!). Our ability to train the dog to use instinct for our benefit, or to achieve "command over instinct," is based on domestication of the dog—the desire to please the handler or "alpha" (predominant) person within the dog's life. This desire to please the handler is an important part of the herding dog. By letting the dog know when you are pleased or displeased with his actions, you will gradually be able to guide your dog's natural instincts, and to use these instincts and abilities to work *for* and *with* you while working stock.

If your dog does not respect and/or trust you, it may appear that he does not want to please you. Establishing the consistency and degree of leadership necessary to establish trust and respect and, thus, the desire to please are vital aspects of handling your stock dog. To the herding dog, respect and devotion are one and the same!

Think of quiet power in the handler as an extension of your authority over your dog. This means that you are able to use a quiet but authoritative tone of voice to communicate.

2

Preparing the Handler and the Dog

"Being ignorant is not so much a shame as being unwilling to learn to do things the right way."

Benjamin Franklin

OVERVIEW

Certain commands are traditionally used to tell the dog how to approach the stock, which direction to take or how to manage the movement of the stock. Knowing these commands and terms is important in communicating with your dog and with other people about herding.

In addition to learning these basic commands, you also need to be able to understand how your dog thinks. Understanding dogs, their reactions to situations and their responses to training can be an intriguing, lifelong pursuit. Each dog is an individual from which you can learn.

Important concepts for training include understanding the dog's behavior as part of a pack; the tendency of dogs to continually test you; the establishment of yourself as the "alpha," or dominant member of the team or pack; the need to set boundaries for behavior and how best to teach your dog. It is important to be able to have the dog follow commands and take correction with a good attitude, and to develop mutual trust and quiet power. Your voice, its pitch and intonation, and your body language are important tools for developing and maintaining this quiet power. Boundaries for acceptable and unacceptable behavior, as well as pitfalls of losing your temper, will be discussed in this chapter. Perspectives on handling problems and personality types in dogs and handlers will also be introduced.

The majority of your dog's herding training must and should be done while working stock. However, some commands and responses should initially be taught prior to work with stock and/or away from the stock. These commands and responses will be useful in generally handling your dog, whether working stock or not. Your dog's responses should become so ingrained that she will respond automatically. Your dog should learn to pay attention when you say her name and should learn the basic commands: ''Lie Down,'' ''Stay,'' ''Here'' and ''That'll Do.''

As a group, each breed of dog has general characteristics typical of their herding style and behavioral tendencies. Certain breeds may be more suitable for certain handler types. Some breeds require different approaches to training. A brief description of a variety of herding breeds with which I have worked is presented here, in order to give you an idea about what you might expect from your herding dog and the training approach that is usually required for a given breed. However, because of the variations within the breed, each dog should be analyzed as an individual in executing the techniques and tactics to carry out your training plan.

HERDING COMMANDS AND TERMS

Traditional Herding Commands

You and your dog will be able to communicate using a relatively standard set of commands. These commands tell the dog to start or to stop and whether to approach the stock by moving straight toward them or by swinging around one side of the flock or the other. Commands are used to indicate which direction to swing or circle (clockwise or counterclockwise), how fast to go and how far out from the stock the dog should be. Other commands may indicate that the dog should move directly away from the handler or go farther back to find an additional sheep or group of sheep. Some commands may be given in combination or in rapid sequence to place the dog at any location with respect to the handler and the sheep.

Below are the essential stock dog commands, in their most commonly used forms, along with explanations of their uses.

"Lie Down"—used as a stop command, to drop the dog in a prone position. This command may be replaced in later stages of training by *"There," "Stand," "Stand, Stay" or "Stay"* in order to have the dog stop on her feet in a standing position.

"Stay"—tells the dog not to move from the stopped position until a countercommand is given.

"Walk In," "Walk Up" or "Go In"—used to move the dog straight toward the stock. Variations of this command may be used to slow down or speed up the dog's approach to the stock.

"That'll Do" or "That Will Do"—used to release the dog from whatever phase of work she is in and call her off the stock. This command usually means that the dog should come to the handler and remain in the area to be available to work the stock again at any time. "That'll Do, Here" will call the dog off the stock and to you.

"Come Bye" or "Go Bye"—used to direct the dog to swing in a clockwise direction around the stock; this clockwise movement is also referred to as being "off the left hand" of the handler.

"Away to Me" or "'Way to Me"—used to direct the dog to swing in a counterclockwise direction around the stock; this counterclockwise movement is also referred to as being "off the right hand" of the handler.

"Steady, "Take Time" or "Time"—used to tell the dog to approach the stock or move around the stock more slowly; this is particularly useful when the stock or circumstances are producing anxiety in the dog. I prefer to use "Steady" instead of "Take Time" because it has a more methodical and calming sound, rather than an anxious tone.

"Look Back"—used when the handler wants the dog to go farther from the handler in order to gather additional sheep that the dog may or may not be able to see; this command may be used with left and right directions to place the dog anywhere the handler desires, for example, "Look Back, Come Bye."

"Go Back"—used when the dog is reasonably close to the handler; directs the dog to go in a direction straight away from the handler.

This is used to relieve pressure when the dog is working relatively close to the stock, such as during penning or shedding.

The above commands are all used as ordinary conversation or requests of the dog, and are not to be used as reprimands (except in cases of severe disobedience). Terms that are mostly used as reprimands—**"Get Out," "Out" or "Get Out of that"**—tell the dog to stay off the sheep or move farther away from the stock, and to work at a greater distance from the stock.

Other Herding Terms

In addition to the above commands, handlers have agreed on other terms to refer to various stages of stock management. Common terms referring to the dog's tasks include:

Outrun—the path of the dog when she leaves the handler and goes to the opposite side of the stock in preparation for bringing them to the handler. The direction of the outrun may be off either the right or the left hand of the handler. Usually the outrun is a semicircular or pear-shaped path. The path of the outrun should keep the dog far enough from the sheep to prevent disturbing them and to ensure that the dog gathers individual stock that may be scattered over a fairly large area of the field.

Lift—the moment of initial contact between the dog and the stock, during which the dog begins the movement of the stock directly toward the handler.

Fetch—the path of movement of the stock to the handler, immediately following the lift. Usually the fetch should be a straight line, and the stock should be moving slowly or at a moderate or controlled rate of speed.

Wear or Wearing—refers to movement of the stock with the handler in the lead and the dog following behind the stock, holding the stock to the handler, in small circles, large circles or straight lines. Early in training you may be walking backward in order to keep an eye on the dog and direct her, as necessary. Later, you may be walking with your back to the dog and sheep, occasionally looking over your shoulder in order to keep an eye on the stock and the dog.

Drive or Driving—refers to movement of stock away from the handler. The dog will be at the rear of the stock, pushing the stock ahead. The relative positions of the handler and dog may change according to the stage of training and reactions of the stock.

Pen or Penning—refers to movement of the stock into a pen or holding area. In trial situations there may be specific rules about the position and actions of the handler and dog to accomplish this.

Shedding or Splitting—refers to separating one (shedding) or more (splitting) head of stock from the rest. These terms may vary in different regions of the country. Traditionally this skill was necessary in order to treat an ill or injured individual or to separate a selected individual or group for market or slaughter. Herding Trials set specific rules about the area in which the shed or split takes place, how it should be accomplished and acceptable actions by the handler and/or dog.

Grip or Gripping—refers to the dog biting or nipping at the stock. In farm work, this action may be necessary to move stubborn stock; at trials this action may be penalized or result in elimination of the dog from competition, if it is deemed inappropriate or unnecessary for a certain situation.

Communicating with Your Dog

Initially, all herding commands are given verbally. In later stages of training they may be integrated with or replaced with whistles. Commands should usually be given quietly and with authority. Your voice should project a tone of *quiet power* to your dog. Generally, there is no need to yell and shout in order to achieve or maintain control. In fact, this may be detrimental since a loud and demanding voice may cause a young dog to get excited and may destroy the quiet and comfortable atmosphere you are trying to produce. By speaking in a soft voice you are teaching the dog to listen carefully to hear you. This gives you the advantage and puts you in control—which is precisely what you are after!

Again, most commands should not be used as reprimands. A reprimand is verbal punishment that expresses your displeasure with your dog. Even a reprimand does not have to be loud to be effective; a lot can be conveyed by a quiet, reprimanding tone. All commands should be taken by the dog with enthusiasm. It is important that, during training, your commands do not come out as reprimands except in extreme cases of disobedience.

Misuse of Commands as Reprimands

One of the commands that is frequently misused as a reprimand, especially by novice handlers, is "Lie Down." The overuse or misuse of the "Lie Down" command as a reprimand may result in a dog that constantly disobeys. When working with a dog that is very intense, this command may be the hardest for you to control.

Commands and Countercommands

Another concept that is important to understand is that of having "commands" and "countercommands." The dog that accomplishes the most is the one that obeys the best! Exceptional control is achieved in part by remembering this: NEVER give a command that doesn't have a countercommand. In other words, if you give a dog a command and simply leave her there, the dog will eventually have a chance to disobey. But, if you give a command and follow it with a countercommand, the dog never has a chance to disobey or break your initial command!

For example, if you give the command "Walk In," you do not mean for the dog to walk in forever. The countercommand for this situation is to say "Lie Down" when the dog has walked in as far as you wanted or *before* she breaks the "Walk In" by blasting into or around the sheep. Being able to give the countercommand ("Lie Down") before the young dog breaks or disobeys the original command ("Walk In") is of great benefit in your early training.

GENERAL CONCEPTS FOR TRAINING YOUR STOCK DOG

The Dog as a Member of the Pack

The dog has evolved from wild canines that lived, hunted and interacted in packs. Herding instinct and behavior are the result of the primitive hunting instinct and the different "jobs" that dogs performed while hunting with the pack. Some dogs were specialists in collecting and moving prey to a location and situation favorable for the kill; some dogs were expert in driving the prey into an ambush; others were more accomplished in separating weak, old or young animals from a herd. All of these components can be identified, to varying degrees, in breeds of herding dogs today.

Within the pack there is a highly organized pecking order, with one individual reigning supreme as the leader, or "alpha." The "alpha" sets the rules and limits of behavior for individuals within the pack. As younger canines mature and become sexually active, the "alpha" must continually reassert and maintain the position as leader.

In domesticated dogs, the social organization of the pack has been expanded to include the people and other animals to which the dog relates within his home or kennel. Ideally, the handler or owner should establish himself or herself as "alpha." It is natural for the young dog, and even the mature dog, to challenge the "alpha" on occasion.

As wild canines rely on the "alpha," or leader, to establish the limits of behavior, your dog relies on you to give structure to life. Rather than being left to her own devices, without discipline, your dog will appreciate and thrive in an atmosphere respecting and being devoted to an individual authority—the "alpha" figure—YOU!

Establishment of the Handler/Owner as "Alpha"

In order for you to establish yourself as the alpha figure in your dog's life, your dog must accept the fact that you have the right and ability to tell her what to do, and she must learn to follow orders. Puppies develop a good attitude toward following orders through general handling and socialization. Puppies should be able to accept being turned over on their back and held gently but firmly until they settle in this position. They should become accustomed to having you handle their feet and toes and look in their mouths. As puppies they are small enough that even a small or weak handler can enforce these procedures. It is more difficult to do in older puppies or mature dogs, since they may have developed strategies for avoiding or disobeying authority.

A good rule of thumb for living with your dog and maintaining your alpha position in either the house or the kennel includes not walking "around" your dog, but making her move if you are walking by or in a direction the dog is blocking. If you continually tiptoe around your dog and do not make her move, the dog may see this as a confirmation of her superiority and position as one who is catered to, rather than as one who must obey. In addition, it is not a good idea to let your dog charge through doors as soon as they are opened, or jump in or out of the car or kennel until told that it is okay. Besides safety benefits, these procedures help acquaint the dog with the need to follow orders and accept them as a part of everyday life. It is useful for every dog to know how to walk on a leash without pulling; to sit, stand and lie down on command; to stay in any position and place and to allow legs, feet and mouth to be handled and inspected, including having toenails trimmed.

Teaching Your Dog

In order to teach your dog these things you will have to be consistent, and you will have to know your dog's tolerance level or "sensitivity to correction." Being consistent means not allowing disobedience to happen without enforcing your authority. Dogs do not understand that circumstances vary; commands should always mean the same thing, regardless of the circumstances.

For instance, if at the park you tell the dog "That'll Do, Here," but allow running around without coming all the way to you, she will not understand that, on the training field, "That'll Do, Here" means to come all the way to you. If you say "Lie Down, Stay" at home, but then you get distracted and do not notice that your dog gets up and wanders off, she will likely feel that it is permissible to break the "Lie Down, Stay" while herding. So when away from or while working the sheep, be consistent with your commands and be ready to enforce them!

Part of enforcing your commands or correcting your dog for mistakes involves your knowing the dog's tolerance level or "sensitivity to correction." In order to enforce your commands you have to fit the punishment to the "crime," and to consider your dog's interpretation of the punishment or correction. For some dogs, a verbal correction, "Uh-uh" or "No," is sufficient. Other dogs may require a physical correction, such as a shake by the scruff of the neck or a jerk on the collar, in addition to the verbal correction. Most dogs will not need more correction than has been explained here. Only the "hardest" dogs that have been allowed to have their own way and get out of control would ever need more correction than has been explained. Be careful always to read your dog carefully; do not correct more than necessary.

A physical correction should make enough of an impression on your dog that you will be able to see it register—she may change expression or have a drop in countenance that will show you the correction is understood.

Following Commands and Taking Correction with a Good Attitude

In order for the dog to take correction with a good attitude, it is important that you make sure your correction is of the appropriate severity, followed by *instant forgiveness*. If you continue to berate or scold after a correction, or hold a grudge about it, your dog will quickly develop a bad attitude toward commands and correction. Once the dog has been corrected, you should get back to work immediately. This usually involves having the dog attempt the exercise or command again. If so, face this as a totally "new" experience. *Do not scold* or withhold your genuine approval just because the dog's *previous* attempt was not successful.

Trust

Trust is a two-way street. There is the trust you have in your dog and the trust that your dog has in you. Trust is extremely important on the training or trial field or on the farm. As the "brains" of the outfit, you must make sure that your dog has a basis for trusting you. A dog who trusts you is more likely to do what you ask, and your trust in your dog will grow as a result.

Your dog will learn to trust you only if you show that you are trustworthy. For example, trust is built by using balance in early training to teach and to help your dog succeed in using instinct *and* doing what you want. If you continually ask a dog to stop off balance early in training when all instincts are warning her that the sheep will escape (and worse yet, if they *do* escape), your dog has learned that you can't be trusted to help make her comfortable. The dog will assume that you are not too bright about the sheep, and therefore you should not be relied upon to know what you are doing!

Increasing your dog's trust in you is a matter of developing your positioning and timing—being in the *right place* at the *right time*. This is why I continually stress the development of your handling skills. Understanding the basis for your dog's reactions and *why* certain things happen is the cerebral part of the formula; developing the necessary skills and abilities through practice is the physical part of the formula.

If you continually set the stage with situations in which your dog has little or no chance of success, then there is an equally low probability that you will be able to develop the trust between you that is necessary for successful training. Later in training, your trust in each other will have been established and your dog will learn to do what you ask, even if it does not seem to make sense or goes against instinct. One of your most important goals in early training is to build trust between you and your dog by creating a sound foundation of training.

Quiet Power

Ideally, you and your dog should each project an attitude and style of working that I refer to as "quiet power." I like to think of quiet power in the handler as an extension of your authority over your dog. This means that you are able to use a quiet but authoritative tone of voice to communicate with your dog. If you resort to yelling and screaming and losing your temper, your dog will feel the tension and anger in your voice, and the situation may promptly escalate to a level of confusion, havoc and panic, from which it is difficult or impossible to recover. Cultivating a demeanor of quiet power will help transfer a quiet, confident and powerful attitude to your dog and create the atmosphere of quiet, calm working that is not only impressive, but necessary for getting the best performance from both you and your dog.

Quiet power in the dog is manifested by her ability to move stock calmly and confidently, without unnecessary roughness or excessive expenditure of energy for the job at hand. *Quiet power in the dog is an extension of quiet power in the handler, and is one of the most important elements in training stock dogs.*

The Role of Your Voice in Developing Quiet Power

Use of your voice is a basic tool in the development of quiet power. Obviously, your voice must be used to verbalize the commands. A more subtle, and often overlooked, aspect of communication is the use of intonation in speech. Like humans, dogs are highly sensitive to the tone of your voice, as well as the subtle changes in pitch and stress that help give meaning to your words. The controlled use of pitch and stress in your voice is critical in every phase of dog training and handling.

Fortunately, the foundation for your dog being "tuned in" to these elements of human language has been laid by her mother. If you observe a bitch licking and soothing her litter, you will hear soft, high-pitched sounds from her as she cleans and bonds with her puppies. A few weeks later, when the puppies are getting too rough and she wants some peace and quiet, the bitch will give a low-pitched growl. Sometimes this disapproving growl is accompanied by taking the puppy in her mouth and clamping down firmly to make the vocal message very clear. In extreme circumstances the bitch may use a very sharp growl/bark to get a rapid response from the pups.

Knowledgeable dog trainers capitalize on the vocalizations of the bitch, using high-pitched, soothing words or sounds to show affection toward and approval of their dogs. Conversely, they will use a low-pitched voice register, almost a growl-like utterance, to express disapproval.

Stress is a feature of language that alters slightly the meaning of words. It helps us emphasize parts of our speech and is associated with change in voice pitch. For example, a drawn-out, soft and low-pitched reprimand, ''Get Out,'' would send a much different message to a dog (or human) than the same words uttered quickly in a higher pitch.

Although these language features are often subtle and may seem inconsequential, they are essential in communicating effectively with dogs. Competent handlers are fully aware that commands and reprimands are effective not simply because of the words used, but also because of the way in which these words are delivered.

Some women may experience more difficulty in using appropriate pitch variations because their vocal pitch range is higher. They may find that they have to practice lowering their voices, or resort to more physical gestures, in order to achieve the maximum effect.

Implicit to the concept of ''power'' is the ability to make things happen or to initiate action. If appropriate use of your voice is not achieving the desired effect, you must enforce your words with physical actions to make an impression upon your dog! Part of enforcing your words involves developing convincing and appropriate body language and delivering physical corrective actions when needed.

Developing Appropriate Body Language

Another essential element of quiet power is development of body language. It is important that your body language, gestures and voice function in harmony when communicating with your dog. When you need to correct your dog to work in a particular way, all of your communication faculties must work together to express that intent. If, for example, you want your dog to work farther from the sheep and you say ''Get Out'' while standing passively with your arms down at your sides, the inexperienced dog will receive a mixed message and either be confused or unconvinced. Instead, in this situation, you should aggressively take a step toward your dog, slapping the crook on the ground, being firm in voice and gesture.

It is important that your body language, gestures and voice function in harmony when communicating with your dog. When you need to correct the dog to work in a particular way, all of your communication faculties must work together to express that intent.

Use of aggressive body language is a calculated element in a training program. *The degree of intimidation that your body language expresses should correspond to the type of dog you are working.* Development of body language differs from handler to handler and you will have to work until you find out what works best for you. If you are working with a hard dog, you will need to exhibit a high degree of intimidation. You want this type of dog to "duck and run" when trying to take advantage of you. But, if your dog has low self-esteem or is very submissive, you will need to employ very little or only mildly aggressive body language. Start out with *less* aggressiveness than you think necessary, and then become more aggressive as you discover what is needed to get the desired response.

For some dogs, a slap on the ground with the boogie bag or crook is enough to get them to kick out, away from the stock, and be apprehensive about coming in too tightly again. Other dogs may not pay any attention to it.

If you ask your dog, "Lie Down," and you get no response, give a yank on the line and watch the reaction. When you jerk your dog back, is she worried about *you*, or do her eyes never leave the sheep? If the dog's eyes never leave the sheep, this may be the type of dog that you will need to come down on fairly aggressively.

Don't "nitpick" at your dog. This is what I call it when you constantly say something, but nothing happens and you don't enforce it. The most common thing I see is the handler telling the dog to "Get Out" over and over without a response! The dog goes wherever she wants, in or out, usually pushing the sheep all over you!

You *must* enforce the "Get Out." In order to do this, your timing and positioning must be correct so that you can enforce it. If the dog is ahead of you, slapping the bag on the ground may only make her go faster, not widen out. But, if you are positioned correctly between the dog and the sheep and you slap the bag, this will make your dog widen out. Your timing and positioning were right! Certain gestures and actions that people use will work, and others simply will not. Watch other handlers and trainers and observe what they do; then experiment with your dog and see what works. This is something every dog/handler team seems to have to work out for itself. Get aggressive, then quit.

Don't allow your dog to think that she can beat you at your own game. Whatever you do, the dog *must* respond! Every time your dog "beats" you by not responding, a bad habit is on the way to being formed. Every handler gets "beat" once in a while, but you must

It is essential to promote and to maintain good attitude, so don't be afraid to praise your dog for a job well done.

make sure that most of the "points" or victories are in your corner, not the dog's.

Promoting a Good Attitude in Your Dog

A dog with a "good attitude" is one that, when being corrected or reprimanded, alters a behavior (learns), but continues to work eagerly and happily. A dog with good attitude does not sulk or pout. It is essential to promote and maintain a good attitude in your dog, and in order to do this, you must make reprimands or corrections severe enough to work, and then make the dog feel good about making the behavior changes. This is usually accomplished by letting the dog go right back to work, but not letting the dog have her own way while working.

A situation that may be particularly important with regard to making the dog feel good about herself is how you approach to catch her just after "blowing her out" away from the stock. Your dog may think you are coming to reprimand her. Your actions, voice and body language must communicate that your dog is going to get patted and praised for doing something right. Keep your eyes on the dog and be ready to react quickly so that you can have her lie down quickly if she starts to get up. Always walk toward your dog in a straight line, maintaining balance, not at an angle that will create an off-balance situation that makes the dog feel a need to move. Once you get close, stand on or pick up the line and *then* pet your dog. That way, if the dog does get up, she won't be able to get away and rebalance on the other side of the sheep.

When you are setting up for an exercise, try to avoid "telegraphing" your intentions to your dog, causing her to anticipate or break premature from position. Dogs are masters at "reading" their human partners. They are naturally attuned to nonverbal cues or body language that tells them what we are feeling and what we are about to do. Dogs know when our verbal messages and body language are not congruent! Establishing trust and being consistent help immeasurably in reducing the ineffective information that we humans unintentionally transmit to our dogs.

Acceptable and Unacceptable Behavior

If you have never trained a stock dog, it may not occur to you that certain natural behaviors may have consequences that affect a dog's performance and ability to adapt to situations. One thing that I try to be aware of and cultivate is keeping dogs "working" while they are working. The dog should not "take a coffee break" to urinate or defecate, get a drink of water or sniff an interesting smell during working time. Try to give the dog an opportunity to relieve herself or get a drink *before* working time. If your dog does happen to start to relieve herself or take a detour to get a drink while working, reprimand the dog and call her back to work. Then praise as she comes back to work.

This may be a particular problem with laid-back or less-enthusiastic dogs, or with dogs that are very sensitive and are feeling a lot of stress during training. Be aware that some dogs will defecate or urinate as a sign of stress or excitement. This type of dog should not be dealt with harshly. Being dealt with inappropriately is probably one reason the dog is acting this way in the first place. Other dogs will continually or intermittently sniff or may eat sheep manure.

Try to read your dog and figure out the reasons for this behavior. If you are convinced that it is not a result of excessive stress, then a reprimand, followed by praise when she comes back to work, may be necessary to break an undesirable behavior pattern. If you feel that the behavior is stress-related, you should change the way you are training; lighten up, change your pattern of work, go to another exercise, let the dog have some fun and then start to tighten back down.

Losing Your Temper

Difficult as it may be, it is essential that you be in control of your emotions when training your dog. I like to tell people that when they walk onto the training field, they should take their temper and put it in their back pocket. There is no sense in losing your temper with yourself or with your dog. It will only interfere with any learning or training that might take place and may do considerable damage. Losing your temper may undo careful weeks and months of training. Why risk it? I will be warning you about some types of training that absolutely *must* be undertaken with a calm and quiet attitude. As much as I believe in working your dog regularly and frequently, if you have had "one of those days" and can't approach training with the right attitude, then *don't train that day*!

Sometimes "calculated anger" is used to make a point with your dog. By this I mean that you will make your dog think you have lost it, that you are absolutely as mad as can be and that you have become a crazy person. But, although based on a genuine feeling, this anger is the sort that is turned on when needed and turned off just as easily. Remember the following:

"Don't steam. Don't be angry. Don't lose your head. It's the best part of your body." (Jimmy "The Greek" Snyder, sports broadcaster)

Perspective on Handling Problems

As I have said earlier, no perfect dogs or handlers exist. In fact, for many dogs and handlers, true learning only occurs by making mistakes and then solving them. Most mistakes or problems initially arise from the handler's or dog's natural tendencies or instinctual responses to circumstances or situations in which they are not experienced. So, remember that these problems should not necessarily be judged as "bad," but should be recognized as "unsuccessful strategies" or areas that need to be worked through in as efficient a manner as possible. It is important to recognize problems as they occur and correct them as soon as possible. If problems are allowed to continue, and unsuccessful strategies continue to be practiced, they will quickly become bad habits! It is always easier to confront and cure a problem when it initially occurs than to change or cure a bad habit.

Some problems may be prevented by thinking ahead and using what you know or have been taught; other problems are unforeseeable, or a situation may not work out as you think it will. When problems do occur, some may be solved at the time of their occurrence; others require thought, reflection and planning to work through at subsequent sessions. This book is designed to help you recognize problems, to avoid situations that may contribute to problems and to help you address and think through problems and learn from them. The following quotation may help you keep your training problems in perspective and inspire you to keep trying:

"A failure is not always a mistake; it may simply be the best one can do under the circumstances. The real mistake is to stop trying." (B. F. Skinner, American writer/psychologist)

Personality Types of Dogs and Handlers

Dogs, like their handlers, have different personalities. *It is important that your personality and that of your dog complement each*

36

other in order to make training enjoyable for both of you. It makes no sense to have a herding dog whose personality does not fit yours and who makes your life miserable.

While each dog must be treated as an individual, some basic personality types can be defined; chapter 7 of this book outlines some of these categories. If possible, you should review that chapter soon after your dog's first introduction to sheep, or after the first few lessons; your dog's particular personality will form the basis for your entire training program.

If you already have and train a dog that you love and cherish regardless of personality, then by all means continue to work with that dog. But, if you are interested in herding and find that your dog's personality makes it extremely difficult for you to train and/or handle, give careful consideration to whether or not you want to pursue herding with that dog.

When shopping for a herding dog or puppy to train, pay close attention to the personalities of the parents *as they work*! A dog that is an absolute ''love'' in the house may be a terror on the field! Many professional trainers will be happy to help you analyze whether your situation may represent a personality clash or a training problem that can be remedied with consistent work. A reputable trainer will be willing to help you acquire a dog that fits you and your personality.

BASIC OBEDIENCE FOR THE STOCK DOG

The basic commands necessary for directing your dog's movement around stock were listed and defined at the outset of this chapter. However, in the early stages of training, some fundamental commands are most easily taught while the dog is away from stock.

"Lie Down" and "That'll Do"

Teaching the dog to lie down is important, but even more important is to lie down with a good attitude! It must be made clear that lying down is not a punishment, but a command, and that you are pleased when your dog obeys. At the same time, a dog should realize that she must obey.

You must establish that a lesson is working time, not play time. Establishing a working relationship and businesslike attitude in both the dog and handler during early training sessions will be helpful at all levels of training.

Teaching a young pup, of approximately sixteen weeks of age, may require many more repetitions in order to achieve the same level of obedience as an older dog. Teaching an older dog (ten months or older) should take less time. Working with a young pup is usually worth the time and effort in establishing yourself as the "alpha," bonding as a *team*, and establishing the habits that will make a useful dog and pleasurable companion throughout life.

Start with the dog on a leash in an area with as few distractions as possible (definitely no stock!). Some experienced trainers may teach the "Lie Down" while training on the field, but work away from the sheep is recommended especially for all inexperienced handlers or handlers of breeds other than Border Collies.

A snug buckle collar or chain training collar should be used. The dog should not be able to slip out of the collar. If a chain training collar is used, there should not be over 2 to 3 inches of slack in the collar in order to have good control. At first, you will be working next to your dog, either bending over, squatting or kneeling.

You will stand up and remove your hands from the dog as she learns to obey when beside you. Then, you will progress to working the dog on a long line at a distance from you. This will establish the obedience needed for the dog to obey your commands while working stock at a distance from the handler.

Put one hand under the dog's chin, holding the leash very close to where it attaches the collar. While commanding "Lie Down" in a quiet but firm voice, simultaneously pull down on the collar and use your other hand on the dog's back to gently push toward the ground (down) and toward the tail (back). In doing this, you should be able to show the dog what you want by gently putting her into a prone position.

After getting the dog into the prone position, don't let her get up immediately. Pet and praise your dog, helping her form a good attitude toward the command. This also teaches acceptance of praise without breaking the command, a tool that will be helpful in other phases of training as well.

If your dog tries to get up, gently put pressure on her back and collar, repeating the quiet but firm command "Lie Down." The dog should stay in the prone position until you feel she is ready for a countercommand. Early in training this may require you to be kneeling beside your dog with your hands in position on the collar and the back, in order to maintain the prone position. As the dog begins to understand, you may gradually remove your hands from the dog and leash, ready to replace them immediately if the dog moves. Eventually you should be able to stand up alongside as your dog remains lying down.

Countercommands

As soon as you feel the dog relax and appear to be content to stay lying down, you are ready for the countercommand. Say "That'll Do," and gently pull your dog to her feet. Pet and praise, just as much as when you praised the dog for lying down.

The sequence of lying down and then giving the countercommand ("That'll Do") should be repeated until the dog starts to respond with less and less physical pressure. Continue until no physical pressure is needed, varying the time the dog stays prone until the position can be held for up to several minutes *before* the countercommand is given. It is especially important during these early lessons to reinforce the "Lie Down" command just before the dog starts to break or get up without a command. This timing is important because the dog has *thought* about standing up just before moving to do so. Therefore, if "Lie Down" is repeated at the time a dog is *thinking* of moving, but before she actually moves, the lesson is made easier because you do not have to deal with actual movement of the dog!

Become an astute enough observer to read your dog's mind and watch for clues in posture, expression or muscle tension that will alert you to your dog's thoughts. This will make any battle of wills between you and your dog less severe. Development of your timing is important in order to have this part of the lesson work to its full potential.

The "Stay" and "Here"

Once your dog will lie down on command without assistance and stays down while you stand close by, remove the leash and attach the long line to the collar. Give the command "Stay" and move a few steps away, holding the long line so that the dog cannot escape from the area or avoid a correction for breaking the "Stay." If your dog moves, quickly reposition her in the *original* location, repeating the command "Lie Down, Stay." Again, the timing of repeating the command "Stay" just *before* the dog moves (while or just after she *thinks* about moving) is critical in speeding the learning process. Gradually increase the distance that you move away from the dog. You should be able to move away in any direction for several minutes at a time. At first, always return to the dog to give the countercommand "That'll Do."

As the dog progresses in understanding and responding to the commands, give the countercommand from a distance. It is a good idea to call your dog *all the way to you* quite often—"That'll Do, Here." This teaches to look for any subsequent commands that may follow "That'll Do." Allowing the dog to wander or run off after each "That'll Do" command would lead the dog to think that the command means freedom to do whatever she wants. Always keep the long line in hand or close by, so that when you need to re-establish contact and control, you can do so with a jerk if needed. Establishment of the dog's attention and immediate response to the handler will be helpful in all phases of stock work.

"Lie Down" at a Distance from the Handler

At the same time the dog is being taught to stay down at a distance, she needs to learn to get up and lie back down at a distance from the handler. One way to do this is to go for a walk on the long line, allowing the dog to get a short distance away from you (without pulling) before giving the command "Lie Down." If she does this well, keep extending the distance from which you give the command. If you reach a point where your dog does not obey as readily, bring her in closer and practice at that distance until she seems to feel secure with the commands. If the dog does not obey the commands readily, give the line a quick jerk and give the command again; make sure your correction makes an impression! The degree of severity needed will vary with each dog and handler combination, but when you get no response, the dog should understand that you are not pleased. She should feel some discomfort if you have to jerk the line in order to get her to lie down.

Try never to go up to your dog to enforce the command; try always to make it happen from a distance, since you will need this control once you start distance work. You must remember that the battle lines are drawn wherever you draw them. If your dog makes you come closer to enforce a "Lie Down," then that is where the battle line is drawn and basically where it will stay. *To avoid this, make the dog lie down from a distance.* For some dogs, a change in the handler's expression or posture will be sufficient to show displeasure; for others, considerable physical force may be necessary, such as a jerk on the collar. Remember not to raise your voice. You will want to save loud commands for times of emergency or severe disobedience when working stock, so use all your resources to get a response to a quiet command at this stage of training.

Breed Behaviors

Some breeds of dogs may resist lying down; they may feel that lying down is very degrading to them. However, this does not negate the fact that they must learn to lie down. Breeds other than the Border Collie may require considerably more training and work to get a reliable stop either by lying down or standing. Later, when working stock, they may be encouraged to stay on their feet (stand), rather than lie down.

SYNOPSES OF HERDING BREEDS, THEIR GENERAL CHARACTERISTICS AND APPROACHES TO TRAINING

Australian Kelpie

This is a gathering breed that shows some "eye," that is, intense stares at the stock, and is usually intense while working stock. They tend to have a high degree of natural ability and must be trained with a quiet but firm approach.

Australian Cattle Dog

This is a driving dog that is usually quite powerful. They may be "pushy" during training. Many are quite talented. They usually need a very firm but understanding approach to training.

Australian Shepherd

This is a driving dog. Certain lines are quite talented and show sustained interest in working stock. Other lines may be easily distracted. The training approach must be matched with the individual, varying from quiet and firm to very light and encouraging.

Bearded Collie

Usually a gathering dog, most are very intense and may bark a lot during the early stages of training. They may be very argumentative and require very firm handling, tempered with an understanding of their sensitive natures.

Belgian Malinois

Usually a driving dog, with tendencies toward gathering, these dogs are usually very aggressive. They may grip (bite) harshly and the handler should be ready to protect the stock. They require firm handling and must be backed off the stock quickly.

Belgian Sheepdog

Usually a gathering dog and very keen, these dogs have a tendency to be aggressive at first, but seldom cause damage. Usually these initial tendencies are easily overcome with training. Initially they must be dealt with firmly but sensitively; later training may require a lighter approach.

Belgian Tervuren

Usually a gathering dog, these dogs tend to show a flash-in-the-pan attitude, coming in aggressively at one moment, but then wanting to leave the stock and look around the next. They may show initial tendencies toward gripping. They require sophisticated handling with great sensitivity to the dog's nature and the ability to be firm when needed and encouraging when necessary.

Bernese Mountain Dog

These are drover-type dogs. They may lack intensity, resulting in a *lack* of *sustained* interest in working stock. They seldom, if ever, grip and must be handled with great enthusiasm in order to encourage sustained interest.

Border Collie

These are gathering dogs that show eye and that, as a breed, usually show a lot of natural ability with stock. Some lines may show a much more laid-back manner and less enthusiastic approach to stock. When training these dogs, the handler must be firm but fair.

Bouvier des Flandres

Usually these dogs prefer a driving style, but may be readily taught to gather stock. They have tendencies to be extremely aggressive toward stock and must be handled accordingly. They may resist direction by the handler and prefer to do things their own way. Training requires a very firm hand and an aggressive attitude combined with fairness and understanding.

Briard

Usually a driving dog with tendencies to play instead of work with the stock, these dogs may show a flash-in-the-pan attitude in which they may come in very hard one minute and fail to show sustained interest the next. They may have a tendency to grip. The handler must be prepared to be aggressive toward aggressive actions, but ready to be encouraging if and when the dog appears to lack enthusiasm.

Catahoula Leopard Dog

Generally a heading dog, these dogs usually show a lot of nerve, stamina and intensity in their approach to stock. Some strains may show a lot of ability. They are quite often aggressive with stock. Training requires a handler with an understanding of the natural style of this type of dog, and as always, the handler must be firm but fair.

Collie—Smooth and Rough

Generally a gathering dog with tendencies toward a flash-in-the-pan attitude of moderate intensity one minute that is easily distracted the next. Seldom aggressive, sometimes quite capable, they must be trained with a lot of enthusiasm in order to keep them feeling good about themselves on the field.

English Shepherd

Usually a gathering dog, this breed contains lines showing varying degrees of intensity and ability. Some individuals may be very aggressive when working stock, but most are not. They must be trained with a great deal of understanding and a firm but fair approach.

German Shepherd Dog

These dogs usually show tendencies to gather more than to drive. Some of these dogs may show harsh gripping. The handler must always be ready to protect the stock. Often they show sustained interest and moderately high intensity. They should be trained with a firm, sometimes aggressive, but *always fair* approach.

Old English Sheepdog

There is a mixture of driving and gathering tendencies in this breed. Some individuals may be aggressive and intense, while others may have a low degree of intensity and lack of interest in stock. They must be worked as individuals because of the variation that occurs within this breed.

Pulik

These are generally driving dogs that are not aggressive and show varying degrees of desire to work stock. They must be trained with an upbeat attitude that expresses constant encouragement to the dog.

Rottweiler

Generally a gathering dog, most have the desire to work. They are less aggressive on stock than one would think, although they should be watched carefully in order to protect the stock. Your approach to training should be firm. You should be alert for any signs of stress since these dogs may, on occasion, be fairly sensitive.

Shetland Sheepdog

Mostly gathering dogs, certain individuals may show a preference to drive. Overall, this is a sensitive breed, and most show a desire to work. Some strains show a high degree of natural ability. Although many start out barking, most quit barking as they settle into working. The handler should be sensitive and responsive to the dog's sensitivities.

Welsh Corgi (Cardigan and Pembroke)

These are driving dogs. Certain strains show a lot of desire to work. Males quite often may be easily distracted by other dogs. Training requires the handler to be extremely upbeat and enthusiastic in most cases.

If you want to know prior to purchasing if a pup of 16 weeks or so has the instinct to work, it may be that you will want to start the dog at that time. There isn't anything much more thrilling than watching a young pup work stock!

3

Introducing Your Dog to Stock

"There are four parts of self that lead to success. The first part is discipline, the second is concentration, the third is patience and the fourth is faith."

George Foster, Major League Outfielder

OVERVIEW

The initial introduction of the dog to stock is very important. It forms the basis for all of your subsequent work, and, therefore, should be an enjoyable and productive experience for all parties involved! Being prepared and having an organized plan will help make the introduction of your dog to stock a positive experience.

Observation of style, tendencies and attitude of your dog during his initial exposure to stock will help determine your approach to subsequent training.

INTRODUCING PUPPIES TO STOCK

There are almost as many recommendations about the age to start puppies and how to work them as there are trainers and breeds of dogs.

I feel that most dogs are not mature enough to handle a regular training program until they are approximately ten months of age, but there will be considerable variation between breeds and individuals within a breed.

If you have a breed that matures early or a breed that may be very harsh or aggressive as an adult, it may be beneficial to start your dog as a puppy. Or, if you want or need to know if a pup of sixteen weeks or so has the instinct to work prior to purchasing him, it may be that you will want to start him at that time. There isn't anything much more thrilling than watching a young pup work stock!

However, starting training early can cause you problems. A pup of a breed that strongly desires to work stock will want to continue to work stock. This dog may want to sneak off, and may go over or under fences in order to find stock. You have awakened a "sleeping lion" that must be dealt with until old enough to progress in a regular training program. But, as long as you are having fun, it certainly will not do any harm to start early. It may, however, be very detrimental to future training if you try to stop your dog from working once having started.

I do not expect puppies to do anything other than have a good time! I may work them once every week or so. In addition, I make it a practice to catch them at the end of the session, pick them up and carry them off the field so that they will not have any negative associations about being pulled from the field on a leash. Most trainers feel strongly that once you start a puppy, you should continue working regularly, even if only once a week.

INTRODUCING THE YOUNG OR MATURE DOG TO STOCK

Few dogs will be mature enough for a standard training program prior to ten to twelve months of age. To introduce the young or mature dog to stock, I prefer to be prepared for any possibility. You will not know whether your dog has instinct or ability prior to introduction to stock or how the dog may react. Consequently, I recommend starting all dogs basically the same way.

Be sure your dog is wearing a flat buckle collar with the 15-to-20-foot nylon long line attached (see chapter 1). You should have three to five dog-broke sheep, and if you are an inexperienced handler or are starting a breed other than Border Collie, you should start in a round or oval pen.

For the introduction to stock, be sure your dog is wearing a flat buckle collar with the 15- to 20-foot nylon long line attached.

If possible, start with a dog that knows the "Lie Down" command when away from the sheep. It is possible to start a young dog without a "Lie Down," but it is more difficult. Be aware that your dog may have a good "Lie Down" before seeing sheep, but may not initially respect it when starting to work. Your ability to stop your dog with a "Lie Down" command may deteriorate into nothingness once starting to work the sheep, because you no longer have quite the authority you did before the dog discovered those sheep! Later you will be concerned about re-establishing *your* authority. But, for the initial session, be lenient and prepared to have little authority when the herding instinct is first expressed.

GOALS OF THE FIRST INTRODUCTION TO STOCK

During the introduction of your dog to stock, your **major goal** will be to try to get the dog to **circle the stock**. You will want to allow the dog to pick the direction initially—clockwise or counterclockwise—and then try to switch the direction of the circle several times during the lesson. The entire lesson will last a maximum of ten minutes.

A **second major goal** is to make working stock **an enjoyable**

experience for your dog and to observe characteristics and tendencies that will influence your approach to subsequent training.

PROCEDURE

Positioning of the Dog, Handler and Sheep

Have a friend hold your dog while you go to the center of the pen or field with the sheep. Place yourself between the dog and the sheep and have a crook or boogie bag in your hand (see Diagram 1). Be careful if you start off with a boogie bag—if your dog is more sensitive than you realized, it may "shut him down" (turn him off of working sheep) in a hurry!

DIAGRAM 1 - Positioning of the Dog, Handler and Sheep when Introducing Your Dog to Stock. The handler is between the dog and the sheep, facing the dog.

If possible, have an older dog bring the sheep up close to you. Or use a little grain to get the sheep close, so that the young dog does not have to "scrape" the sheep off the fence.

Then, have a friend let the dog go. Your job is to block the dog from coming straight in toward the sheep. If your dog wants to come straight in, take your crook or boogie bag and swish it along the ground in front of you so that it makes a little noise and causes the dog to think twice about coming straight into the sheep. Use a distinct swinging motion so that the dog has to bear either left or right when coming in.

If the dog wants to go clockwise around the sheep, let him go clockwise; if he wants to go counterclockwise around the sheep, let him go that direction. *Let the dog pick the direction.*

Encourage the dog by saying "Good dog." Some people say that talking to a dog encourages him to direct attention to you rather than to the sheep. But in training hundreds of dogs, I have never found this to be so. Usually, if the dog is keen enough to work in the first place, talking to him is unlikely to cause the dog to be distracted and look away from the sheep. If the dog is distracted and looks up at you and wags his tail, it is likely that you will have a hard time keeping this dog on the sheep, regardless of what you do. The dog will not know whether he is doing things that are "good" or "bad" until you enforce the "bad dog" with some reprimands and reinforce the "good dog" with praise. Once you reinforce these terms, your dog will learn the difference.

Remember to use a quiet voice to talk to your dog while he is working. A soothing sound should be used to convey "Good dog." A low-pitched, stern voice, similar to a growl but more powerful, should be used to say "Get Out" if the dog is too close to the sheep.

Position and Use of the Crook While Circling

Let's say that the dog has gone clockwise around the sheep. You also should go clockwise around the sheep. You should be slightly to the rear of the dog and between the dog and sheep, in a sense "following the dog," forcing him to stay out on a larger circle (see Diagrams 2 and 3). You are walking or jogging around the sheep and your dog is running in a circle. It is like a big wheel—the dog is the rim, you're the spokes and the hub is the sheep turning in place.

If your dog is circling *clockwise* around the sheep, your crook

DIAGRAM 2 - Positions of the Dog, Sheep, Handler and Crook While the Dog Is Circling the Sheep Clockwise. Your dog is circling the sheep clockwise. You follow the dog around the circle, staying off the dog's hindquarter. The crook is in your left hand and is used under the dog's neck or slapped on the ground to help keep the dog out and away from the stock.

should be in your *left hand*—the hand closest to the dog. Your body and the crook should not inadvertently come out in front of the dog. If they do, the dog may quickly change directions at a time when you are not prepared for it. The crook can be slapped on the ground to keep the dog out from the sheep, or it can be slipped under the dog's neck and used to push him away from the sheep, making a larger "wheel." Only in the most extreme circumstances, such as if the sheep's health is in jeopardy, should the dog ever be hit with the crook.

Changing Direction of the Circle

After the dog has gone around two or three times in the clockwise direction, you should turn around and walk into the face of the dog

DIAGRAM 3 - Positions of the Dog, Sheep, Handler and Crook While the Dog Is Circling the Sheep Counterclockwise. Your dog is circling the stock counterclockwise. Your crook is in your right hand as you follow around the circle, pushing the dog out and away from the sheep.

to get him to change the direction of the circle (see Diagram 4). You will switch your crook from your left hand to your right hand as you turn to walk into the face of the dog, so that again the crook is toward the outside of the circle. Step away from the sheep just a little bit as you do this and try to block the advancement of the dog. If the dog does not change direction the first time you "meet" him, just keep walking and try again when he comes around to meet you the second time.

Walking into the face of the dog is usually the easiest method of changing the direction of the circle. But if you have a dog that works a good distance from the sheep, you may be able simply to cut across

You should be slightly to the rear of the dog and between the dog and sheep, in a sense "following the dog," forcing him/her to stay out in a larger circle. You should be walking or jogging around the sheep while your dog is running in a circle. It is like a big wheel— the dog is the rim, you're the spokes and the hub is the sheep turning in place.

If your dog is circling clockwise around the sheep, your crook should be in your left hand (the hand closest to the dog).

After the dog has gone around two or three times in one direction, you should turn around and walk into the face of the dog to get him to change the direction of the circle; keep the crook toward the outside of the circle.

the circle and head your dog off so that he changes direction (see Diagram 5). Then let the dog go in this direction several times before attempting to change the direction again.

Importance of Continuous Movement

It is important that you *do not allow the dog to establish a balance point on you*! You must keep on the move so that the dog will keep on the move and keep reading you and reading the sheep. If the dog succeeds in establishing a balance point, the sheep will stop moving. It is likely that your newly started dog will not be able to tolerate having them immobile, and will come in and "blow them apart"! The dog may grip (bite) while doing this. Only a mild correction should be used at this time. Remember that the dog is only following instincts, and you as the handler have let this happen because you have allowed the young dog to establish a balance point. You must keep moving in a circle to give the dog something to do. If your dog closes in, try to step toward the dog and push him out. Keep in mind that this is the dog's introduction to sheep; do not come down too hard. This is a

DIAGRAM 4 - Changing the Direction of the Dog Circling the Sheep by Changing the Direction of the Handler's Movement. If you desire to change direction while the dog is circling the sheep, do a 180 degree turn and walk in the opposite direction to meet the dog. As you turn, switch your crook to the hand toward the outside of the circle, slapping the ground to block the dog. If your dog does not change direction the first time you meet him, keep walking and try again when he comes around the next time.

critical time and if you shut him down with too many inappropriate reprimands, it may take *weeks* to get your dog started again!

Instead of insisting that the dog be blown out early on, I recommend allowing the dog to be tighter than you normally would want, as long as you can keep him off the sheep.

Ending the First Lesson

During this first lesson you will switch the dog's direction several times so that he goes a few times around the sheep first one way and then the other. The entire lesson should not last more than ten minutes. After you have gone around several times and have changed direction several times, then either have your dog lie down (if he will!) or move

DIAGRAM 5 - Changing the Direction of the Dog Circling the Sheep by Cutting Across the Circle. If working at a good distance from the sheep, your dog may be guided to change direction by you cutting across the circle and blocking the dog's progress. As you cut across the circle, switch the crook to the hand that will be toward the outside of the circle.

the sheep to the fence, and get between the dog and the sheep and catch or step on the long line to stop him. Pick up the long line and call the dog off the sheep by saying ''That'll Do,'' and walking directly away from the sheep (see Diagram 6). Do not try to take your dog past or through the sheep—this would create too much of a temptation to grip at such an early stage of training.

THINGS TO NOTICE DURING THE INTRODUCTION TO STOCK

During the initial exposure of your dog to stock, it is helpful to notice several things that will influence what you do in subsequent lessons. You should try to note whether your dog has natural gathering

It is important that you do not allow the dog to establish a balance point on you! You must keep on the move so that the dog, in this case a Smooth Collie, will keep on the move and keep reading you and reading the sheep.

or driving tendencies, the direction he prefers to go and the degree of intensity with which he watches and responds to the stock. You should try to gauge the degree of seriousness with which he conducts himself—is his tail up and is he barking? If so, this may indicate that your dog is primarily playing. Does the dog seem to be sensitive to pressures, such as changes of direction or movement of the heads of the sheep? Is he very aggressive, wanting to grip (bite), or gentle with the sheep? Is he easily distracted, sniffing or wandering off from the stock? Is your dog worried about whether or not he is pleasing you?

How, you may ask, can I tell if my dog has driving or gathering tendencies when I am trying to get him to circle the sheep? Detecting these tendencies requires recognizing subtle differences in the position of the dog while he is circling the stock. The *gathering dog* will tend to be to the periphery or outside of the sheep, holding them together. The *driving dog* will tend to fall in behind the sheep as they and the dog go around in a circle.

Almost all dogs will have a preferred side. They will prefer to circle in one direction or the other. Just like most people are either right-handed or left-handed, dogs may be more comfortable going to the left (clockwise—a "left-handed" dog) or to the right (counterclockwise—a "right-handed" dog).

DIAGRAM 6 - Calling Your Dog off the Sheep. To call your dog off the sheep, make sure you pick up the end of the long line, say "That'll do" and walk directly away from the sheep. Your dog should not have to go through or around the sheep in order to get to and go with you.

It is important when you first start a dog to determine which side the dog prefers. This is the side you will work the *least*! The more quickly you can "balance up the dog," that is, to run either side equally well, the better. He should feel as good about going clockwise as counterclockwise. This makes for a better dog that will be able to progress more rapidly in all training.

The Balanced Dog

Developing a balanced dog makes sense, if you think about it. Think of a baseball batter who is ambidextrous (able to bat either left- or right-handed). Few players start off this way. If they are naturally right-handed and also want to bat left-handed, they force themselves to bat left-handed until they are comfortable with it. Likewise, force your dog to go in the uncomfortable direction until he becomes comfortable with it. This will not happen during the first lesson, but will occur gradually as you continue to work.

To determine whether your dog prefers to run clockwise or counterclockwise, observe the reactions of the dog and how closely he works to the sheep when going in each direction. Usually a dog will work closer to the sheep while running in the direction he is most *uncomfortable*. It will likely be much harder to get your dog to circle at all in the uncomfortable direction. He may be more inclined to grip going in the uncomfortable direction as well.

You might think that being uncomfortable would make a young dog go farther out and *away* from the sheep, but this is not the way Nature works. Instead, Nature determines that, when a dog gets in close, the "kill mechanism" is triggered and the dog would be able to have "dinner" (if he were out in the wild). Those dogs that are uncomfortable going one direction have to be *taught* to kick out and away from the sheep. In some individual dogs, there is a natural instinct to kick out and get off the sheep, to establish a natural comfort zone.

Because situations arise very rapidly with an inexperienced dog and handler during these introductory sessions, it may be of benefit to have a friend observe from the sidelines to help you perceive these tendencies in your dog.

These are some of the elements I try to assess at the initial evaluation of any dog. Other individuals, groups or sponsors of herding instinct evaluations may assess a variety of other factors, including whether the dog barks and how much. I have found some of these factors (especially the barking) to be highly variable and not to have much effect on subsequent training. I do not recommend that the handler reprimand dogs for barking. Most dogs that initially bark do settle down and work quietly after they have some training and have decided to work.

PROBLEMS THAT MAY OCCUR DURING YOUR DOG'S INTRODUCTION TO STOCK

Problems that may occur while introducing your dog to stock include:

1. **Inability to get your dog to go in one direction or the other.**
   If you were unable to change the dog's direction of movement or it was very difficult to change direction and/or he came in *very* tight in one direction, you may have a "one-sided" dog.

   Dogs show varying degrees of one-sidedness. To get the *extremely* one-sided dog to go in the nonpreferred direction, there are several things that you can try.

Remember that you are using balance, your positioning and your crook—all the training aids at your disposal to help accomplish this task. You may have to put yourself extremely off balance or *overcompensate* in terms of balance in order to get your dog to go in the desired direction. You may also need to use the crook aggressively and *slap* it sharply on the ground, to get him to go around *and* to back him off from the stock. Backing the dog off from the stock in his nonpreferred direction will help him grow more comfortable with this direction of movement, and will help prevent gripping that may be associated with his initial discomfort. Some solutions:

a. The first thing you can try is to place yourself extremely off balance to the dog to compensate for his disliking a particular direction (see Diagram 7). This may require stepping further to the side or away from the sheep than would be necessary with less one-sided dogs.

b. If putting yourself extremely off balance to the dog does not seem to work, try to back up to a fence with the sheep between you and the dog. Let's say your dog is very uncomfortable going clockwise (see Diagram 8). Your dog will

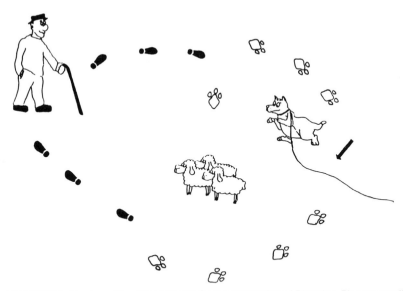

DIAGRAM 7 - Forcing a One-Sided Dog to Go in a Nonpreferred Direction. Place yourself extremely off balance to the dog to compensate for your dog's dislike for a particular direction.

DIAGRAM 8 - Using the Fence Line to Force a Dog in an Uncomfortable Direction.

want to go in a counterclockwise direction around you, but the fence prevents him from getting around you. You will step to your left (the dog's right) and ease around in a clockwise direction. As you ease around, your dog will become so uncomfortable about the sheep possibly trying to escape that he will swing away from you in the clockwise direction.

As soon as he starts to move, make sure that you are quick to get out and away from the fence—back up a few steps—to allow the dog to come on around the sheep, giving the sheep some space to move. Also, be quick to get around behind the dog and follow him around the circle, being very encouraging at the same time, so that you can keep the dog going in this nonpreferred direction for three to five turns.

c. If your dog stops and refuses to go in this nonpreferred direction, then you may have to "pull the sheep around him" (Diagram 9). To do this, envision placing yourself so that the dog is the hub of the wheel, the sheep are the spokes and you are the outside rim. This is the *opposite* of what we are usually trying to achieve, but may be necessary to get your dog started in the nonpreferred direction.

As you walk around your dog in a clockwise circle, keep slapping your crook until he eventually becomes so uncomfortable that he will go clockwise. Once the dog starts to move, be ready to follow around and help him understand what you are after.

If your dog is *extremely* one-sided, this problem will not be overcome in a single lesson, week, month or even a single year. It requires a lot of work and patience to overcome extreme one-sidedness. This is not meant to discourage you, since most one-sidedness can be overcome rather quickly. But if you do have a very one-sided dog, this

DIAGRAM 9 - Pulling the Sheep Around the Dog to Get the One-Sided Dog to Go in the Nonpreferred Direction. To pull the sheep on around your dog in the direction that he does not prefer to go. Place yourself so that you represent the outside rim of a wheel, with the sheep as the spokes and the dog as the hub. As soon as your dog starts moving in the uncomfortable direction, be quick to follow around the circle and keep the dog going.

aspect will be one with which you will have to deal repeatedly throughout his training

2. **Unable to get dog to "Lie Down."** If your dog forgot the "Lie Down" command while being introduced to stock, be patient, and do not be afraid to *repeat* the "Lie Down" command. Make sure that you are exactly on balance with your dog before attempting the "Lie Down" command. If you can line yourself up directly opposite your dog so that you hold the "point of balance," or block as your dog tries to go one way or the other to get at or go around the sheep, you will usually be able to stop the dog. *Once stopped, many dogs will become attentive enough to lie down on command.*

It may help to practice the "Lie Down" and "Stay" while *away* from the sheep to make sure of your dog's foundation and understanding of the command. For the initial exposure, you may have to back up to a fence and catch the dog by stepping on or grabbing the long line. Be lenient about expecting instant obedience during the early stages of training, during which your dog is trying to resolve the conflict of obeying two masters—you and his instincts. Don't expect your dog to lie down and stay for long periods. Once the dog lies down, either catch him or go back to work *before* he breaks the "Lie Down."

When trying to catch your dog, be aware that you may be leaving the sheep exposed and he may try to dive in and grip at that moment. It may help to have a friend help you catch the dog. Some dogs may come to you if you step between them and the sheep and talk to them softly and coaxingly.

3. **Dog does not seem interested/does not "turn on."** Remember, not all dogs will "turn on" the first time they are exposed to stock. Some breeds, particularly if they have had a lot of obedience training, may be reluctant to leave the handler or are not sure that this is *really* something that they should be doing! If you discourage them at all during their initial encounters with stock, it is as if they say, "I *knew* this was too much fun to be right. I'd rather please my master than obey my instincts, so I just won't work stock!" You have to be extremely upbeat and encouraging to get these dogs to realize that working stock is what you want.

To encourage this type of dog, use a *sh-sh, shoo-shoo, ch-ch-ch* sound to "shoosh" or "hiss him along" and get your dog excited. This sound is not like anything dogs may have been exposed to as a command in the past, and it usually helps get them excited. You may have to get right up on the sheep and pat them to encourage the dog to get close to them. It may help to catch a sheep and bring the dog up close to sniff it.

Sometimes it helps to have someone else move the sheep around and see if the movement will provide some excitement for the dog. Sometimes removing the long line will help if the dog has had a lot of Obedience work when on leash. You may have to try and make working stock a "game" for your dog. If a dog does not show interest at the first exposure to livestock, it is always prudent to try again at later dates.

Dogs who have been well trained in Obedience may need more help in beginning to focus on the sheep instead of solely on the handler. To solve this problem, keep the sheep between you and the dog. As the dog tries to get to you, you should continue to circle away, and without realizing it he may begin to work the sheep, gradually shifting attention from you to the stock.

Give your dog ten minutes or so of honest encouragement. See if he begins to show some tendency to move toward the sheep, watch the sheep or move after them. Be very careful, while trying to get your dog to work, that you do not put too much pressure on, causing him to quit for good. It is usually better to work for less time and more frequently in order to increase this type of dog's intensity. Repeating the exposure to stock may help get the dog to turn on. If he still shows no interest, he may not have much or enough instinct with which to work.

4. **Dog wants to grip.** Don't be so tense about your beginning dog biting a sheep that you yell or overcorrect him to the point that the dog turns off. If your dog is extremely aggressive and really wants to grab, hold on and/or bring a sheep down, then you will have to be aggressive also and yell, slap the crook and stay between him and the sheep. But if he is just interested in grabbing a little wool or a flank as he goes by, be lenient during the first few exposures, tell your dog to "Get Out of there" and get him to let go as quickly as you can.

   In *subsequent* lessons, it will be important to let the dog know that grips are bad in order to keep gripping from becoming a bad habit. But, at the initial exposure, try to avoid discouraging the dog in any way!

You should try to change the direction of the circle after the dog has gone around two or three times in one direction. At this point, it is very important to get the dog to start working on *you*, holding the sheep to the handler, rather than all of your directions being focused on keeping the dog away from them. In order to do this, keep the sheep between you and the dog.

4

Beginning Herding Training

"Have patience. All things are difficult before they become easy."

Saadi, Persian poet

OVERVIEW

The initial exposure to livestock has helped you determine whether your dog has the instinct to herd. Hopefully you have been able to observe some characteristics, such as preferred direction of movement around the stock, herding style and some elements of personality type, that will guide you as you plan your dog's training program. You are now ready to begin a program for herding training for you and your dog. An important part of your work at this level will be *teaching yourself and your dog* the basic commands and terms for working sheep.

In the beginning stages of herding training you and your dog will be learning how to use balance, to establish and maintain a "comfort zone," and to "read" the sheep and each other. You will also review the basic commands, presented in chapter 2, which will direct your dog through these early training exercises.

GOALS OF BEGINNING WORK WITH
THE NOVICE DOG

Your goals for this stage of working are to

1. get the dog to work on you, not just on the sheep
2. begin to get the dog to look to you, as the "alpha," for leadership. These first two goals are important in getting the gathering dog to work both *on you* and *for you* and in getting the driving dog to work *for you*.
3. establish the basic commands and exercises used in training your dog; this will involve using command associated with instinct, as well as the beginnings of establishing command over instinct
4. maintain a good attitude in your dog and yourself
5. begin developing the bond and teamwork necessary for you and your dog to form a working partnership

Both inexperienced and experienced handlers will want to be aware continually of reading the dog, the stock and the situations so that training can proceed with as few "accidents" as possible.

FIRST LESSONS AFTER THE INITIAL
EXPOSURE TO STOCK

The next few lessons will use the same format as described for the initial exposure to stock. Start these next lessons with the dog circling the stock. You will try to change the direction of the circle after your dog has gone around two or three times in one direction. At this point, it is very important to get the dog to start working on you, holding the sheep to the handler, rather than all of your directions being focused on keeping the dog away from them. In order to do this, keep the sheep between you and the dog. You should gradually begin to stop the dog more frequently, remembering to ask her to drop only when *on balance*. You will ask your dog to circle most often in her nonpreferred or uncomfortable direction.

As the dog is on the way to the opposite side of the stock from you, you should sometimes "give ground" or move away from the sheep, letting the dog move the sheep toward you in a straight line as she comes to the point of balance. Do this only for very short distances at first. As the sheep are moving toward you, you will start to move around them, again backing in large circles, to encourage the dog to hold the sheep to you while she maintains proper distance.

It is a good idea for inexperienced handlers to start using the directional commands (''Come Bye'' and ''Away to Me'') when the dog is moving in the appropriate direction. By repeating them as the dog moves around, the dog will come to associate the commands with movement in a particular direction. Also, and probably most importantly, *you* will begin to learn the correct command for the direction of movement and will be able, with practice, to direct the dog using these commands! I have had inexperienced handlers tell me that it takes them a long time to be able to tell the direction of movement and be able to respond immediately with the correct directional command. So, start early!

Getting the dog to work at an appropriate distance from the sheep, getting her to slow down and establishing a reliable stop are all related. The dog will be more inclined to stop reliably when out from the sheep, maintaining a comfort zone. But often it is hard to teach where that comfort zone is without having a good stop! The dog will not feel so much pressure once maintaining a comfort zone is learned and, therefore, will tend to slow down and be easier to control. However, it is hard to get the dog to recognize the comfort zone without being able to slow her down. Each is dependent upon the other. Have patience! You eventually will get there!

DEVELOPMENT OF HANDLING

In the initial lessons you have been encouraging the dog to circle the stock as a relatively controlled way to work around the stock and express instincts and abilities. Now you should be ready to eliminate the circling over the next few lessons. You should now have enough control to stop the dog as she gets to the opposite side of the stock, to have the dog change directions when it is *your* idea (not hers) and to swing your dog around the stock and bring them to you over a short distance.

You should be refining your ability to recognize when the dog is on balance, meaning when the dog, handler and sheep are comfortably aligned (see Diagram 10). The actual positions of the dog, handler and sheep at the balance point will depend on the pressures involved.

DIAGRAM 10 - Stopping the Dog on Balance. During the early stages of training, you should be careful to stop your dog on balance. The alignment of the dog, handler and sheep that results in stopping all movement represents the "constitution of balance" or "reaching a balance point." This diagram shows a point of balance that results in the handler, dog and sheep being aligned along a straight line. If other factors such as gates, fences, other sheep, or other dogs are active, the point of balance may shift.

Remember, from the dog's point of view, balance has been achieved when she has stopped all action and you, the sheep, and the dog are stationary.

You should begin to be able to recognize pressure points and to read both the dog and the sheep. You should notice what makes the sheep move and how the dog reacts to these movements and to your commands. For example, before the dog starts to move, the sheep will often watch the dog, but sometimes will watch the handler. As the dog and sheep start to move, anticipate the direction of movement of the sheep by watching their heads—they will move in the direction their heads are turned or the direction they are facing.

Try to anticipate your dog's actions and reactions to the changes in the movements of the sheep. Watch your dog's expression, carriage and speed. It is easier to stop the dog *just before* she takes off *than while* charging through the sheep. It is easier to ask the dog "Walk In" toward the sheep *before* breaking a "Stay" than to be angry at her for breaking a "Stay."

Anticipating sheep's behavior is the key to controlled, smooth movement in future work in confined areas and in trials. It takes considerable experience and practice to become proficient in this handling skill. Focus consistently on developing this skill in yourself as you train your dog.

Common pressure points that may influence sheep movement include:

1. The gate—once the sheep know the location of the entrance/exit to the pen or field, they may preferentially congregate there or move more rapidly when headed in that direction. They may be more difficult to move away from the gate.
2. Other sheep—sheep never seem satisfied! Wherever they are is not where they want to be! The presence of other sheep in an adjacent area may draw the sheep toward them.
3. Other dogs—the presence of another dog may discourage sheep from moving in a certain direction. This may be used to your benefit if sheep are extremely "sticky" or sullen by a gate or some part of the working area: Have a handler or a friend with dog on leash quietly stand in that area. But be aware of potential problems if you are *trying* to move sheep toward an area where another dog is present.

"GET OUT" AND "STEADY"

When told "Get Out" while swinging around the sheep, your dog should turn *away* from the sheep (kick out) 90 degrees or better (see Diagram 11). It is important for the dog to do this correctly. This is the very earliest start of "square flanking," or establishing the ability of the dog to work consistently at the desired distance from the stock, without creeping or cutting in as she works.

"Steady" is the command used to slow the dog's approach to the sheep. It is extremely important that you be able to control the speed of the dog. If the dog is moving rapidly, the sheep will tend to move faster and faster. This can cause you great difficulty! Making turns and

DIAGRAM 11 - The "Get Out" Exercise. To set the stage for the "Get Out" exercise, start with the sheep between you and the dog. Have your dog lie down at the balance point. Then, step to one side of the sheep and tell your dog to "get out." Your dog should kick out and maintain a radius from the sheep equal to the distances he was originally placed from the sheep. You may stop when your dog reaches the balance point behind the sheep, or you may let the dog fetch the sheep to you.

stopping a flock of sheep can be done with precision only if the sheep are moving at a reasonable speed.

I start using the "Steady" command right from the beginning. Any time the dog starts to move too quickly, I repeat the word "Steady" over and over in a firm but quiet tone. Then I have the dog lie down as quickly as possible. This helps confirm the meaning of the command. (Remember, the "Lie Down" should not be used as a reprimand!)

It is important to remember that the dog seldom can be "steadied" overnight. It takes a fairly long time (days to weeks) for a dog to grasp what is wanted. Many factors cause this, one of which is a keen desire to work sheep, which can make a day "pushy"! At this point in training, she will not have relinquished the control needed to be fully committed to slowing down.

Slowing down is a progressive accomplishment and must be approached carefully so that the dog doesn't become discouraged with the whole idea of working stock. Being pushy at this stage does not mean being disobedient. This is simply reacting to instinct. Only through consistent and planned training can instinctive responses be controlled and modified without being lost completely.

Possible Problems with the "Get Out" and How to Handle Them

If the dog does not "kick out" when told to "Get Out," you probably are not being forceful enough with your "Get Out" reprimand and need to slap the boogie bag or crook harder to reinforce the verbal command. Try to position yourself between the sheep and the dog when you give the command, so that you are at the balance point and the dog cannot beat you around the sheep. Or you may be allowing the dog to go too far around the sheep and away from you before commanding the dog "Get Out." Try to stop her sooner and then say "Get Out." Don't let your dog go all the way around the sheep or cut in on them before being told to stop and "Get Out" again.

You may have misread the type of dog with which you are working. If she swings quickly, the dog may have a tendency to be excessively pressure-sensitive (see chapter 7) or may be more keen or intense than you thought. Or your dog may have a much harder personality than you thought. You may have to build yourself up to a "calculated anger"; you may have to act ferocious once or twice and then back off. You simply can't allow the dog to take over!

When told to "Get Out" while swinging around the sheep, your dog should turn *away* from the sheep (kick out) 90 degrees or better.

"Steady" is the command used to slow the dog's approach to the sheep. It is extremely important that you be able to control the speed of the dog.

"Wearing" refers to the movement of sheep, with the handler on one side of the sheep and the dog on the other, "Holding" the sheep to the handler. This may be introduced while still working in the small round or oval pen, or in a larger field.

You may have created your own problem by allowing the dog to take over and beat you once or twice. So you must regain that ground you lost!

INTRODUCING WEARING

"Wearing" refers to the movement of sheep, with the handler on one side of the sheep and the dog on the other, "holding" the sheep to the handler (see Diagram 12). This may be introduced while still working in the small round or oval pen, or in a larger field.

To start wearing, leave your dog on a "Down, Stay" on one side of the sheep and position yourself on the other side of the sheep, facing the dog. Begin to walk backward, keeping an eye on your dog. When you have established a comfortable distance (which varies with each dog and set of sheep) between the dog and the sheep, tell your dog "Walk In." It is important at this point that your tone of voice be quiet and calm, to help not to excite the dog. You may have to call her name and say "Come In, Here" at first in an encouraging tone to get the dog up and moving. Be sure then to say "Walk In" so that she learns this command. "Walk In" means she is to move straight toward the sheep, without going around to head them off or to circle them. If your dog starts to come around you to head the sheep off, just step toward the same side that she is trying to come by and snap your crook on the ground, at the same time saying "Get Out."

Walking backward is difficult for some people, but it is important that you do so to keep your eye on your dog and encourage or discourage him appropriately. Be aware of uneven terrain or obstacles that may sabotage you! Even experienced handlers, while backing up, may suddenly end up on the ground with the sheep and then the dog continuing right over them! Later, after the dog has learned to hold a proper comfort zone, you will be able to turn around and walk facing forward.

Initially you will want to wear in a large circle, switching directions frequently. You may wear around the periphery of the small pen or work in a circle in the middle of a larger field. If the dog comes in too fast or the sheep begin to move past you, stop the dog, establish some distance or change direction and start again. This will help teach the dog to balance on you.

If the dog seems to be doing well when wearing in small and large circles, try wearing in figure eights, alternating changes of direction. In the middle of the figure eight, start doing short, straight lines. If the

DIAGRAM 12 - Wearing. To start Wearing, you will be backing up with the sheep between you and the dog. You should stop your dog if the sheep are moving too fast or moving past you. Your crook should be switched from hand to hand and/or slapped on the ground, as needed, to keep the dog behind the sheep. Your dog should maintain a constant distance from the sheep while Wearing, not cutting in on turns while wearing in a circle, or while doing figure 8s or serpentines.

dog gets edgy, then start turning again. This way she will learn to start coping with wearing in straight lines. Remember that the crook is a training aid, and should be positioned so as to keep the dog in proper position behind the sheep.

Remember to break up your wearing, sometimes letting the dog swing around the stock—as long as she does not try to swing around past you. Some dogs may become bored with wearing for too long a period when it is first introduced. This may result in a dog coming up behind the sheep and "blowing them apart." This creates some excitement for the dog, and if this is a dog with some degree of natural ability, she may then gather the sheep back into a group. Other intense (keen) or super-sensitive dogs may try to grip and hang onto a sheep as it goes down the field, or split a sheep off from the flock.

If this happens, try to get the dog to let go of the sheep by commanding firmly "Get Out of that!" You can try to have the dog lie down, but usually dogs will not respond properly in this situation. So slap your crook on the ground and try to get the dog to the outside of the single sheep, so that that sheep can head back toward you and the rest of the flock. When the dog gets to the outside and the sheep is headed back to you, be sure to praise and say what a good dog she is! Even though the dog created the problem in the first place, all of a sudden she is doing it right—and bringing that sheep back to you!

Any tendency to cut into the middle of the sheep must be corrected quickly, and you must always be alert to avoid any recurrences. Remember, this will usually happen when you haven't given dogs enough to do by keeping them moving or turning.

Always start wearing while turning. Gradually, the size of the circle can be increased and figure eights and serpentines can be added so that your dog is wearing for longer periods and with more gradual turns and short, straight lines. Eventually, you will be able to back up in a straight line along the fence or in an open area for longer and longer distances.

If you feel your dog is working well at a distance and you are confident with your ability to control the dog and the sheep, it may be time to move to a larger field. The time and number of lessons spent in the small oval pen will depend on both the dog and the handler. It is advantageous to move to a larger field as soon as you feel confident enough to do so, since you can teach the dog to work at a distance with less crowding of the handler by the sheep.

With some dogs, like most Border Collies, you will want to be out of the small oval pen within a lesson or two unless your sheep are very wild or unless you have very little confidence in your dog. Otherwise, you may be doing more harm than good by staying in that small area.

Possible Problems When Introducing Wearing and How to Handle Them

Possible problems when introducing wearing include:

1. **Dog comes in too close.** I cannot emphasize enough that your dog must be taught as quickly as possible to stay off the sheep! As you swing the dog around the sheep, step between the sheep and your dog, slapping the ground with the crook as you command "Get Out." If you try to stay on the other side of the sheep, you can't accomplish this as easily.

   Your dog must learn "Get Back," "Get Off" or "Get Out." If she knows this, she will kick out or turn at 90 degrees or more to go away from the sheep while starting to swing around them. (Refer back to Diagram 11.)

Your dog may want to be a little "pushy" because of a keenness to follow instincts. But at the same time, your dog may be very sensitive to your verbal corrections. This can create a challenging problem that is intriguing to try to work through. You have to get the dog to do what is right, but do it in such a way as to leave your dog's self-esteem intact and keep her enthusiastic and happy about working.

What you have to do, a lot of times, is to get tough and make your point, then lighten up and make everything easy and active for your dog. Then clamp down again, then lighten up again; this way, the dog will learn to take orders from you, but also will learn that the world does not come to an end when she is corrected. Many dogs will shut down if you come down hard, trying to get what you want all at once. But if you don't come down hard enough, your dog will be all over the top of you, having her own way!

After you back her off, you will be able to see that the dog will begin to understand about holding the comfort zone and will stop when you stop without having to be told to do so. If she will do this, your dog is maintaining the comfort zone and you have accomplished what you are after!

2. **Flopping back and forth.** This refers to erratic side-to-side swinging of the dog behind the sheep while wearing. Take into consideration the number of sheep you are working. If you have a large number of sheep, fifteen or twenty, your dog may need to move from side to side a little to keep the corners "tucked in." But if you are working a smaller number of sheep, five to ten, the dog *must* learn to wear in a straight line. Except with very large numbers of sheep, there should never be total side-to-side motion.

If your dog is following the sheep too closely, she is more likely to flop back and forth in order to get a perspective on the overall group, as she is able to do when farther back. It is like looking at a painting at a museum. If you stand up close you may have to move from side to side to see all parts of the picture. If you stand farther back you are able to see the entire picture without moving from side to side.

Some dogs naturally "flop." Strong-eyed or talented dogs often wear to one side or another of the sheep if they are very pressure-conscious. It's up to you to get the dog back behind the sheep where she belongs. It may help to work parallel to

If you have a large number of sheep (15 or 20), the dog may need to move from side to side a little during wearing, to keep the corners "tucked in."

a fence so that you only have to guard her from flopping on one side. Keep the "worst" side next to the fence.

To help keep the dog in the comfort zone, be sure to use the "Steady" command. Instead of saying "Walk In," call your dog's name. This may make her less likely to try to come around or close to the sheep. You may have to have your dog lie down while you move the sheep away. But don't always rely on "Lie Down" to stop her back there. She should learn to hold a Comfort Zone independently, without always being told to lie down. If she starts to come in too close, say sternly, "Get Out of that, you. What's the matter with you? Now, Steady." This may cause your dog to check and learn to stay back. When this is learned, your job will be much easier!

If you constantly have to use commands to tell your dog what to do, you may be on your way to creating a "push-button dog" that does not retain the ability to think independently and keep working on her feet.

3. **Dog tries to "head" the sheep or come around past the handler.** The excessively pressure-sensitive dog, the intense (keen) dog or the talented dog with a lot of natural ability (see chapter 7) may tend to work on the heads of the sheep, rather

than on the handler, during early training; this also is true of some dogs with strong driving tendencies. You must deal with this problem immediately! Like any problem, it is easier to deal with it as soon as it is recognized. Problems are habit-forming. *Good training is developing good habits!*

For example, let's say that you are wearing, backing up while facing the sheep and dog and the dog tries to come around past you by swinging in a clockwise direction, up on your right side. Step to your right, in front of the dog. Slap the crook on the ground and command "Get Out" or "Get Back." Stepping over in front of the dog will be more effective than using the crook alone, since you will be creating an off-balance situation. In addition, you are now in a position to create the desired counterclockwise movement. Once the dog gets back behind the sheep, praise with "Good dog."

If she tries to come around on the other side while swinging back, step to your left, with your crook in your left hand, and swing your dog back behind the sheep again. Then, use "Steady, good dog." If you continue to do this, she will learn to stay back behind the sheep and steady.

4. **Dog won't "Lie Down."** Don't let "Lie Down" turn into a debate—the dog must comply quickly, but while still maintaining a good attitude. If you have a dog that is quite sensitive to pressure, that wants to beat you and not lie down, you will need to take whatever measures are necessary to stop this! You may have to back up to a fence so that she will be less likely to try to go around and around the sheep rather than lie down.

   If you have a laid-back or strong-eyed dog (see chapter 7), one that wants to "clap" or lie down quickly and too frequently, you may need to keep this dog on her feet and constantly working, using few or no "Lie Down" commands. If, on the other hand, you have a very keen dog, you may have to be more demanding. Remember to ask the dog to lie down *only* when on balance. But don't let your dog push you all over the field. Use a lot of power, but be fair; read your dog! Demanding obedience today may detract from the natural ability that you desire in these dogs in the future.

5. **Dog won't "Walk In."** A good rule of thumb for teaching the "Walk In" is to take advantage of the time when you are

walking out to the sheep. You will have your dog on a long line; try to keep the line loose, not tight. A tight line is simply a crutch—the only thing it teaches a dog is that a rope doesn't break!

As you approach the sheep, tell your dog "Lie Down." Be very quiet. Tell her "Walk In" as you walk toward the sheep, giving a gentle tug on the long line if she does not get up. Puppies, once they get up, may want to take off immediately. Be ready! If your dog does this, tell her to lie down quickly. Your dog may hit the end of the rope going full speed. Immediately tell her to lie down again. Once she's down, then say "Walk In, Steady." Of course, you will not want to do this until after you have worked your dog several times. Even then, don't do it to excess—just three or four times on the way out to the sheep. This starts the seed growing that helps a dog understand "Walk In."

The strong-eyed dog may want to stay down and not walk in. If so, call her name, then "Here, Here." Once your dog is up, praise with "Good dog" and then "Steady."

Once your dog has learned "Walk In," she may want to move in faster than you want. "Walk In" is associated with a fast approach. So change the words! Don't use "Walk In"—use "Here, Come On," a name or whatever will work to get her up. The dog will be hesitant because of not being sure what you want. Quickly say "Steady" so she will understand that slow movement is what Steady means.

If she is coming in too close, say "Lie Down." Your dog may not actually lie down, but will check herself. Don't worry about making the "Lie Down" stick. Let it go and just say "Steady." Later, you will be able to go back to "Walk In" and will be able to steady your dog. This technique breaks the habit of coming in too fast.

BALANCE EXERCISES

While wearing, you can keep your dog from getting bored and help teach the dog to balance on you by doing what I call balance exercises. These exercises are the Walk Through (see Diagram 13) and the Walk Around (see Diagram 14).

82

DIAGRAM 13 - Balance Exercise: The Walk Through. To do a Walk Through, begin by backing up with the dog Wearing the sheep. Then, walk forward through the sheep and to one side. Your dog should respond by swinging around the sheep to reestablish balance. You will pivot 180 degrees to watch the dog. The sheep will be turned by the dog. Then you may stop the dog on the far side of the sheep or back up to continue Wearing.

DIAGRAM 14 - Balance Exercise: The Walk Around. To do the Walk Around, start out backing up, with the dog Wearing the sheep. Then walk forward and around one side of the sheep. Your dog should respond by swinging around the sheep to reestablish balance. You pivot to watch as your dog swings around the sheep. The sheep will be turned by the dog. You may stop your dog on the far side of the sheep or back up to continue Wearing.

To do the **Walk Through** balance exercise, you start by backing up, with the dog wearing behind the sheep. Then walk forward and through the middle of the sheep, toward your dog and slightly to one side. Your dog should swing around the sheep, away from you, in order to get back on balance.

For the **Walk Around** balance exercise, start the same way—backing up with the dog wearing behind the sheep. Then stop backing up and move forward and around the side of the sheep, toward the dog. The dog should swing to the opposite side of the sheep in an attempt to balance on you.

The direction the dog swings around the sheep will depend on the side from which you approach. These exercises are usually done with a minimum of commands. But if you are just learning the directional terms, say the command as your dog swings around the sheep; this will help *you* learn the commands. Remember to make sure your dog holds the working radius while swinging around the sheep when doing these exercises.

Possible Problems with Balance Exercises and How to Handle Them

1. **Dog flies in and grips.** Your dog needs to go back and learn "Get Out" in order to stay *off* the sheep. You may be dealing with a problem that reflects extreme discomfort when going in one direction if the dog is very one-sided. If so, you may need to be fast—once the dog starts around the sheep, you must run between the dog and the sheep to keep her off the sheep, slapping the crook and saying "Get Out."

2. **Dog does not go in the expected direction.** Again, this may reflect a very one-sided dog. You may need to place yourself *extremely* off balance to the dog in order to get your dog to go in her nonpreferred direction. Make sure that you are positioning yourself properly and that you have your crook in the hand toward the outside of the circle, ready to block if the dog should try to come past you in the wrong direction.

3. **Dog goes wider and wider to evade the handler and keeps going the way she wants.** This situation may require you to step away from the sheep and run as fast as you can across a diagonal path to head off and get the dog going the way you want. Sometimes getting closer to a fence so that she cannot

get past you by going wider will help, as recommended previously for the one-sided dog. (Refer back to Diagram 8.)

THE "GET OUT" EXERCISE

This exercise helps teach your dog to move farther out or away from the sheep. You have already used "Get Out" to make the dog move farther from the sheep while circling. This exercise reinforces that command and helps dogs learn to respect the "Get Out" command in different situations.

For the "Get Out" exercise, start with the sheep between you and the dog. Flank the dog in either direction. For this example, let's say you send the dog in a clockwise direction. You then need to step over toward the dog, maintaining your own distance from the sheep and dog. Your crook will be in your left hand and out to your left side. As your dog turns to maintain balance, say "Get Out" in a firm tone. At this time, the dog should turn out away from the sheep, at an angle of 90 degrees or better. (Refer back to Diagram 11.) For this exercise, the "Get Out" is the primary command, and the direction commands "Come Bye" and "Away to Me" are secondary. Later, when you are concentrating on teaching directions, the directional command will be the primary command. Once the dog gets to the far side of the sheep, then have her lie down and set up the exercise again. Make sure you do this exercise in both directions. It will be more difficult for the dog to get out and away from the sheep without cutting in while going in the nonpreferred direction.

I prefer to use "Get Out" instead of "Get Back," since I use "Go Back" to get the dog to move directly (180 degrees) away from the sheep. *Commands that sound too much alike may add confusion* to the training process.

TEACHING DIRECTIONAL COMMANDS

You will have been using directional commands ("Come Bye" and "Away to Me") as your dog moves in the appropriate direction so that both you and she can learn the commands by association with the desired movement. In order to imprint these commands more strongly and help your dog learn them, you also will want to practice swinging your dog around the sheep, starting her from the "Lie Down" (see Diagram 15).

Begin by having your dog lie down. You will be between the sheep and the dog, facing your dog. In order to get your dog to swing in the counterclockwise, the "Away to Me," direction, move to *your* right, the dog's left, holding the crook in your right hand out to the side and slightly toward the dog. This places you off balance to the dog. In order to balance, she *must* move in the counterclockwise or "Away to Me" direction. In setting your dog up this way, you have assured that she will succeed!

Then gently slap the crook on the ground and give the command "Away to Me." It may be that you will have to move slightly toward the dog on a counterclockwise circle to create some movement that will encourage her to move. As she swings around the sheep in the desired direction, praise and say what a good dog this is and then have her lie down when she reaches the other side, or step back and allow the dog to move the sheep to you.

DIAGRAM 15 - The Handler-Between Outrun. For this outrun exercise, you will start your dog in the desired direction from your position between the dog and the sheep. Your crook will extend *away* from the side of the outrun. Your dog should maintain the same distance from the sheep all the way around the outrun.

In order to get your dog to swing in the counterclockwise direction (the "Away to Me" direction), move to your right (the dog's left), holding the crook in your right hand out to the side and slightly toward the dog.

To get her to go clockwise (the "Come Bye" direction), hold your crook in your left hand, extended to the side and slightly toward the dog. Remember always to hold the crook toward the outside of the circle, whichever way you are circling.

To get her to go clockwise, the "Come Bye" direction, set yourself up on the opposite side of the dog. You will stand between the sheep and the dog, facing the dog. You will step to *your left* (the dog's right). Hold your crook in your left hand, extended to the side and slightly toward the dog. Gently slap your crook on the ground and give the "Come Bye" command to get your dog moving in the counterclockwise direction.

These exercises will help teach the directional commands rapidly, since you have positioned yourself so that your dog's balance instinct causes her to move in the correct direction. Soon you should be able to get the dog to take direction when you are on the opposite side of the sheep. As she learns the commands, you will not have to move as far to the side (not use such extreme off-balance positioning) and will not have to use the crook as much.

DIRECTIONS WHEN MOVING OFF BALANCE

You also have to teach your dog to take directions when *she* is moving off balance. If the dog only learns to take directions in response to the instinct to balance, you will not be able to get her to move off balance in response to your commands when the need is critical.

Prior exercises have had you position yourself *away* from the direction you want the dog to go. Now you will pull the dog around you to go the direction you desire (see Diagram 16). To set the stage for the dog to move in a clockwise direction, have your dog lie down, with you between the dog and the sheep. Initially you will place yourself only slightly to the right, as you face the dog. As your dog learns this exercise, you will be able to move farther away. This positioning is *toward* the direction you want the dog to go. Your crook will be in your left hand and extended to the side. If necessary, call the dog's name or take hold of the line, forcing the dog to come in your direction. Give the dog the "Come Bye, Here" command. If she does not go in the desired direction, stop immediately and give the line a small jerk to get her attention. Repeat the "Come Bye, Here" command.

A variation of this exercise involves using the long line. Move to your right and one step beyond the dog, so that the dog is between you and the sheep, facing the sheep. Hold the long line in your right hand. Your toes will be facing away from the sheep and you will rotate your torso toward the dog (to the left). Your crook will be in your left

DIAGRAM 16 - The Handler-to-Side Outrun. Handler moves *to* the side that the dog will be sent but a little *past* the dog. The handler will be facing away from the sheep. The handler's body rotates toward the dog, with a crook in the hand *closest* to the dog. The crook should be behind the handler and slightly toward the dog. Ideally, the dog will maintain the same radius all the way around the sheep. If the dog cuts in, the handler may stop the dog. The handler then moves to a new position and starts the dog again.

hand and extended behind you and toward the dog. The long line will be in your right hand and across the front of your body. Tell your dog "That'll Do, Here," giving a slight tug on the line, if needed, to get her started in the desired direction.

As your dog comes to you, sweep your crook along behind, telling her "Come Bye." Use a hiss ("*Sh-h-h-h*") if needed to encourage her to go on around. (Refer back to Diagram 16.) You will want to make the dog go all the way around the sheep, 180 degrees. You may either stop your dog on the far side or allow her to bring the sheep to you. Eventually, you will be able to stand still in the middle of the sheep and just extend your arm or the crook to one side to get your dog to move around the sheep. She should come past you and circle around the sheep as far as you desire when you say to do so. This is a true test of whether or not your dog actually understands the directional commands!

This exercise will help the dog learn to come around past you, moving in an off-balance direction. Once she will go in either direction, have her swing first one way and then the other, going for various distances around the circle, before changing direction. At first you will stop your dog ("Lie Down") before changing direction. Later, you will be able to have the dog change direction without stopping first.

THE "CALL IN"

This exercise helps to solidify your control over your dog, as well as prepare for future tasks. To do a "Call In" you will step between the dog and the sheep. At first you should be only a few feet from her and have the long line in your hand, so that your dog cannot zip past you and blow into the sheep.

Call the dog directly in to you, using her name and "Here." The dog's eyes and attention should be on you, not on the sheep. You may need to step in front to keep your dog from slipping by to one side or the other. You may have to reel in the long line as she comes to you. Once at your feet, cradle the dog's head so that she looks up at you. Repeat the dog's name and say "Here." Be sure to praise both as she comes in and when she looks at you.

At first the dog will be looking around your legs at the sheep. Be patient. Gently, but firmly, cradle her head so that she looks at you. Then call her off, moving away from the sheep. Reposition the dog for another "Call In" or another exercise.

The "Call In" may be lengthened as the dog learns to respond. It is important that she come in immediately and rapidly (at a trot, not a walk). Try to do several during each lesson. Remember to be enthusiastic and encouraging, to maintain your dog's quick response to this command.

THE "GO BACK"

This command tells the dog to turn around and move directly away from the handler (see Diagram 17). It is useful when the dog moves closer to the sheep than desired and is used to relieve pressure.

90

To do a "call in" you will step in front, between your dog and the sheep. At first you should be only a few feet from the dog and have the long line in your hand, so that she cannot zip past you and blow into the sheep. Call your dog directly in to you, using her name and "here." The dog's eyes and attention should be on you, not on the sheep.

It is easiest to introduce the "Go Back" in a fenced alleyway or narrow area, or along a fence that will help your dog understand to go *straight back*. It is possible to teach the "Go Back" in the middle of a wide-open field, but it is easier to teach if you can make an alley that is about 12 feet to 16 feet wide and 20 feet to 80 feet long.

Have the sheep at the end of this alley and walk the dog into it and toward them, but not so close that both the dog and sheep get nervous. Have the dog lie down. You will start out between the dog and the sheep, facing the dog. Hold the end of the line that the dog is dragging so that you will be prepared to help if your dog doesn't understand right away.

Initially, you will be standing toe to toe with the dog, blocking approach to the sheep. Tell the dog "Go Back," emphasizing the word *back* in a quiet but firm voice. If the dog does not get up, you may have to swing the crook or boogie bag in front of her face and/or slap it on the ground in front of her. Make sure the line is short enough so *your dog cannot dart past you and toward the sheep*. If she tries to go to one side, step over so that you stay directly in front of and between the dog and the sheep. If your dog does manage to get past you, jerk her back away from the sheep. Have her lie down and start again.

DIAGRAM 17 - The Go Back. When you say "Go Back," your dog should turn around and move directly away from you until a countercommand is given. You may be between your dog and the sheep *or* on the far side of the sheep.

It is important that the dog go *in front of you*—you should not be leading or dragging the dog behind you. Try to have the line loose. You must initially intimidate your dog to get her to turn her back and leave you and the sheep.

As the dog begins to turn and go back, you should follow her for a few steps. The first time she turns around, have her lie down immediately, saying what a good dog she is. It is important to praise since she was feeling intimidated enough to turn around in the first place! This way she will recognize that "Go Back" is just another command and *not a reprimand*. If she does not face you when you say "Lie Down," call her name until she turns to face you and *then* say "Lie Down." Don't bring the dog all the way back to you, then tell her "Go Back" again. At first you should be happy if she goes back 5 or 6 feet. But by the time the first lesson is over, the dog should be going back for a distance of 15 or 20 feet.

As your dog understands what you want and is beginning to go back fairly easily, it is time to start changing the timing of your praise. Say "Good Dog" as she is going back—don't wait until after you have the dog lie down. This will help a dog realize that the movement *away* from the sheep is what you want. Have her lie down, praising again for lying down.

Once you have driven the dog back several times, bring her back closer to the sheep and start again. After doing this several times, you should try to let some of the line out and have the dog move away *without you following* as closely or as far. You want to be able to stand still and have the dog move away from you as soon as possible. Gradually you will be able to increase your distance from the dog. Eventually you will be able to direct your dog to go back up to 70 or 80 feet (may require repeating command) even when on the far side of the sheep from you.

Once you are fairly confident with your dog in the alleyway, it is time to move out into the field. You may find that the dog will want to swing to the right or left instead of going straight back. If she starts to do that, quickly say "Lie Down," step over so that you are in front and again give the command "Go Back."

This is one of the important terms your dog needs to learn and it will represent a major step in establishing authority over your dog.

"Go Back" with Breeds Other Than the Border Collie

This exercise is extremely important for teaching all herding breeds. Be particularly careful with the other breeds since they may decide once they have left the sheep that they might as well keep going! It is important that they recognize that this is a command, not a reprimand, and that they feel good about themselves while doing the "Go Back."

Possible Problems Teaching the "Go Back" and How to Handle Them

1. **Dog does not turn around and move away from handler.** You may not be aggressive enough or clear enough about what you want your dog to do. Remember, you have to be intimidating enough to get your dog to want to leave you and, for an *instant*, forget about her desire to work sheep.

   You may be positioned too close to your sheep. If so, your dog may be so "locked in" on the sheep that it will be hard or impossible to teach this command. Try giving yourself a little more distance from the stock.

2. **Dog does not go straight back.** It is important that your dog go straight back, so do not let this problem continue! This most often shows up when you move to the large field and your dog no longer has a narrow alley or aisle for guidance. Be ready to stop your dog immediately if she tries to swing in either direction around the sheep. Then step over so that you are directly in front of your dog and command "Go Back" again. Have the long line snug enough that she cannot swing very far to one side or the other. You may have to follow a short distance with a short hold on your line.

DEVELOPMENT OF THE INEXPERIENCED DOG'S UNDERSTANDING OF COMMANDS

Initially, your dog used only instinct when working the sheep. You didn't have the ability to control or command these instincts. As the handler, your goal is to develop the ability to control the dog and to use instincts and abilities to *your* advantage.

The inexperienced dog's understanding of commands initially is based on association with natural instincts and abilities (command associated with instinct). For example, by positioning yourself off balance to the dog, you will cause the dog's instinct to tell her to move in that direction in order to establish balance.

Another area you will want to develop is your ability to use body language to your advantage, to communicate effectively with your dog. If you need to correct your dog, or to encourage working farther away from the sheep, are you using aggressive body actions that correspond with your verbal message? Exactly what you will need to do depends on the type of dog you are training, and what she will interpret as aggressive. You only need the amount of aggressiveness necessary to get the job done.

Aggressive body language is a calculated thing. It needs to be intimidating! The degree of intimidation should correspond to the type of dog with which you are working. It seems to differ from handler to handler, and you will have to work until you find out what works best for you. For example, if you are working with a "hard" dog (see chapter 7: Personality Types in Herding Dogs), you will need a high degree of intimidation. You want that dog to duck and run because she is trying to walk all over you anyway. But if you have a submissive dog with low self-esteem, you will need to have very little or only mildly aggressive body language. Start out with less aggressiveness than you think you need, and then work up from there, as you discover what is called for.

If you ask the dog to lie down and she doesn't do so, give a quick yank on the line and watch the reaction. Is she worried about *you, or* do her eyes never leave the *sheep*? If the dog's eyes never leave the sheep, this may be the type of dog that you will need to come down on more aggressively.

Don't nitpick at your dog. This is what I call it when you constantly say something and don't enforce it. The most common mistake I see is the handler telling the dog "Get Out" over and over and nothing happens. The dog goes wherever she wants, in or out, or all over the field!

You must *enforce* that "Get Out." In order to do this, you must watch your timing and positioning. If the dog is ahead of you, slapping the bag or crook on the ground may only make her go faster but not widen out. But if you are positioned between the dog and the sheep and *then* slap the bag, *this* will make her widen out. Your timing and positioning were right! Certain gestures and actions will work; watch other handlers and trainers and see what they do. Experiment with your dog and see what works. This is something all handlers seem to have to work out for themselves.

Get aggressive, then quit. Don't allow the dog to beat you at your own game. Whatever you do, the dog *must* respond! Every time she beats you, it is a bad habit on the way. Everyone gets beaten once in a while, but you must make sure that most of the points or victories are in your corner, not the dog's.

Watch the dog's countenance. If she kicks out away from the sheep, then you should immediately lighten up and "hiss her along" ("*Sh-sh-shoo*") to get your dog feeling good about herself again as quickly as possible.

PROMOTING A GOOD ATTITUDE IN YOUR DOG

The two most important things to remember in promoting a good attitude in your dog: Make a reprimand or correction severe enough to work, and then make the dog feel good about herself.

One situation in which it may be particularly important to make the dog feel good is walking up to a dog you are ready to catch, after having blown her out and away from the sheep. The dog may think you are coming after her again if you do not change your actions, voice and body language to communicate that your dog is going to get petted and praised for doing something *right*. Don't take your eye off her, and be ready to react quickly. You can use the "Lie Down" quickly if you see her muscles twitch or she even *thinks* about moving. Also, do not walk up to the dog at an angle that will create an off-balance situation, making the dog feel like it is necessary to move. Once you get up to your dog, step on the line and *then* pet her. That way, if the dog does get up, she won't be able to get away and beat you.

When you are setting up an exercise, do not telegraph your intentions before you are ready, causing the dog to anticipate or break from position. To illustrate this concept, I often tell people that they have made the dog think that they are going to "steal her wallet." It is the type of movement that is suspicious and communicates your intent to the dog.

Dogs are experts at reading us! They are naturally attuned to nonverbal cues or body language that tells them what we are feeling and what we are about to do. Dogs know when our verbal messages and body language are not congruent! This is part of establishing the trust and consistency necessary for effective training.

Having the dog "come off the sheep" with a good attitude is important, and she should be praised for leaving the sheep, coming with you and giving you attention.

At this point in training you should not expect the dog to be able to obey instantly in all situations. However, with patience and practice, you will be able to ask your dog to react to commands in situations that require her to pay attention to the command rather than just instinct. This is the beginning of development of command over instinct. As training progresses, you will be asking your dog to obey commands that go against instinct, achieving true command of and cooperation from your dog in a variety of situations, without causing a loss of any instinctual abilities that make a valuable working partner.

You will continue to practice calling your dog off the stock by picking up the line and saying "That'll Do" while walking directly away from the sheep and toward the gate (refer back to Diagram 6), or when you are positioning your dog while setting the stage for a particular exercise. Having the dog "come off the sheep" with a good attitude is important and she should be praised for leaving the sheep, coming with you and giving *you* attention. Later in training the dog may be asked to come off the sheep with "That'll Do" and then immediately start back to work. Establishing a good attitude and good habits at this early stage in training will be of benefit throughout any dog's working career!

The comfort zone varies for each dog and for each group of sheep. In the picture above, the Sheltie can work relatively close to the sheep without disturbing them; in the photograph below, the Belgian Tervuren must hold a much wider working radius in order to maintain the comfort zone.

5

Intermediate Stages of Herding Training

"Don't mistake activity for achievement—practice it the right way."

John Wooden, college basketball coach, UCLA

OVERVIEW

If your dog and you have mastered some *or* all of the exercises in the previous chapter, you are ready to move on in training. It is not necessary to have mastered *all* of the exercises in the preceding chapter in order to progress to intermediate exercises. Some exercises or tasks may be more difficult for you and/or your dog—keep working on these, but continue ahead in those areas for which you are ready.

New exercises and tasks you and your dog will start in the intermediate stages of training include the outrun, lift and fetch, square flanking exercises (maintaining working radius), fence-line pickups and beginning driving.

GOALS OF INTERMEDIATE STAGES OF TRAINING

Your goals for this stage of training are (1) getting the dog to work *on you* and not just on the sheep, (2) refining your ability to work with your dog in a variety of situations and at various distances from the stock, (3) introducing additional exercises and tasks that will contribute to the usefulness of a stock dog and (4) continuing to refine and develop command over instinct. Inexperienced handlers will want to be sure they are continuing in their development as part of the team. Both experienced and inexperienced handlers should always be aware of reading the dog, sheep and situations, and of positioning themselves correctly for the exercises used in training.

WEARING, DIRECTIONAL COMMANDS AND "STEADY"

Continue wearing as described in the previous section, increasing the length of time and distance, with and without stopping the dog. At this stage, you should be able to move the stock in a specific path and direction of movement.

Continue to establish the directional commands. By this time you should be able to decrease the use of the crook and the amount of body language you use to get the desired response. Eventually your dog should be able to take directions from you, regardless of your position in the field. But at this intermediate stage, your dog probably will still require some help in order to understand what you want. Try to give a directional command without moving your body or crook. If the dog does not respond correctly, be ready to stop him or step in with the appropriate movement or use of the crook to help the dog understand.

He should be learning to move more slowly toward the stock on the "Steady" command. Be sure your dog will do this at varying distances from the sheep. The dog should also work at varying distances from the sheep on other commands as well.

INTRODUCING SHORT OUTRUNS, LIFTS AND FETCHES

At the intermediate stage your dog should be ready to start doing short outruns, lifts and fetches. You have actually been doing very

The outrun is the path that the dog takes in getting to the other side of the sheep, opposite the handler. Initially you will be positioned between the sheep and the dog and send the dog in the desired direction by positioning yourself off balance for that direction. This is what you've been doing to teach your dog directional commands and is what I call the "Handler-Between Outrun."

short ones already, when you were teaching your dog directions and pulling him around you!

The "outrun" is the path that the dog takes getting to the other side of the sheep, opposite the handler. Initially you will be positioned between the sheep and the dog and send the dog in the desired direction by positioning yourself off balance for that direction. This is what you've been doing to teach your dog directional commands and is what I call the "Handler-Between Outrun." (Refer back to Diagram 15.)

The "lift" is the initial movement of the sheep following the outrun, as the sheep begin to move toward the handler. The path of movement of the sheep to the handler is the "fetch." Usually you will drop your dog on the opposite side of the sheep and then tell him "Walk In" to start the lift and fetch. This ensures that the lift will be quiet and controlled. If your dog slows down naturally or begins to anticipate the drop, you should practice completing the outrun, lift and fetch without stopping. The distance at which the dog is placed from the sheep, and your distance from the sheep, will increase as you gradually lengthen and widen the outrun.

Another outrun exercise is the "Handler-to-Side Outrun." (Refer back to Diagram 16.) You leave your dog on a stay and move to the

For the "Handler-to-Side Outrun," you leave your dog on a Stay and move to the side where you want the dog to go. Call your dog by name and then "That'll Do, Here," giving a little tug on the line, if needed. Just as he comes to you, follow along behind with the crook and say "Away to me" or "sh-sh-sh-sh" to swing the dog in the counterclockwise direction around the sheep.

side to which you *want* the dog to go. Instead of moving off balance so that the dog moves in the direction to reconstitute balance, you are placing yourself so that the dog *must* first *move off balance* before swinging around the sheep. This is beneficial in establishing command over instinct and being able to work your dog in off-balance as well as on-balance situations.

Position yourself two or three steps to one side and one step beyond the dog for this exercise. If you are not sure that your dog will come to you when called (he might just go straight into the sheep!), then use the long line, gently pulling it to indicate the direction you wish your dog to go.

In order to get the dog to move in a counterclockwise direction ("Away to Me"), you will start between sheep and dog, in front of and facing the dog. You will take a step or two to *your* left and one step forward so you are beside and slightly beyond your dog. Your crook will be in your right hand. Your feet will be facing away from the dog and the sheep (toes located farther from the dog than your heels). You will leave your feet stationary and turn your torso clockwise (to the right), putting your crook behind you and letting the end touch the ground. If you are holding the line, it should be in your left hand.

Now, call your dog's name and then "That'll Do, Here," giving a little tug on the line, if needed. Just as the dog comes to you, follow along behind him with the crook and say "Away to Me" or "*Sh-sh-sh-sh*" to swing your dog in the counterclockwise direction around the sheep. When the dog gets to the other side of the sheep, have him lie down. Walk to the dog, reposition and do it again.

By setting yourself up to the *dog's* left (your right), you can send him in the clockwise or "Come Bye" direction. To do this, start between the sheep and dog, facing your dog. Take two or three steps to your right (the dog's left) and at least one step beyond the dog. The crook will be in your left hand, and your torso turned to the left, or counterclockwise.

It is important to go *beyond* the dog because it is easier for the dog to take attention completely off the sheep and come around you. If you set yourself up between the dog and the sheep (*not beyond* the dog), the dog will be more likely to "cheat" (not come to and around you) since he does not completely have to break concentration on the sheep.

Do this exercise three or four times in a row to make sure your dog knows what you want. He should be coming off the sheep readily to come to and go around you. The benefits of this exercise are three-fold: (1) It provides the first step toward going against a dog's natural instincts or desires—his *natural* instinct when you are positioned to the left would be to go counterclockwise or "Away to Me." Instead, you are positioning yourself to the dog's left, calling him *off* his balance point and then asking him to go in the *off-balance* direction to re-establish balance again on the other side of the sheep. This is important in establishing command over instinct. (2) It contributes to your ability to call your dog off the sheep *and* have him come off with a good attitude. (3) It is another step in establishing the path of a good outrun.

If your dog cuts in (does not make a perfect arc when swinging around the sheep), have him lie down, reposition yourself and start again. This pattern of stopping and repositioning all around the sheep in either direction is the "Daisy Wheel Pattern." It is useful in widen-ing the dog out and for increasing *your control* over the dog. The Daisy Wheel Pattern necessitates stopping the dog in the off-balance position. Be aware that repeated stopping when out of balance may discourage some dogs. Take frequent breaks to encourage your dog to go on around the sheep, or do some wearing or other exercises in order to keep the dog motivated.

The third Outrun exercise is the "Sling-Shot Outrun" (see Dia-gram 19). Leave your dog on a "Stay" and move so that he is between you and the sheep, but closer to the sheep. You should be just *slightly* toward the side that you want the dog to go. Your body position will be the same as for the Handler-to-Side Outrun. Call the dog off the sheep, and give the directional command as he comes to you and swings around you. This exercise encourages enthusiasm and speed on the outrun. It helps widen the outrun as well. The dog can be stopped if he tries to cut in, as described for the Daisy Wheel Pattern. As your training progresses, you should gradually increase the distance between you before calling your dog toward you.

Sometimes the dog should be allowed to complete the outrun, lift and fetch with a minimum of direction from the handler. With enough repetition, the dog will naturally slow at the point of the outrun when he reaches the opposite side of the sheep. The sheep should move off for the lift and fetch at a walk or trot, not an all-out run!

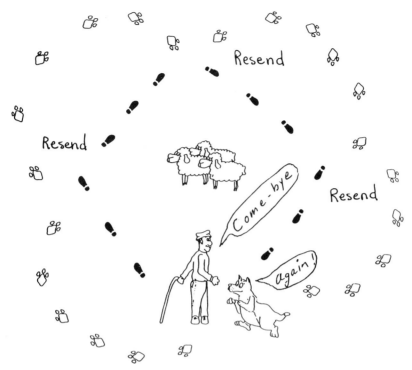

DIAGRAM 18 - Daisy Wheel Pattern. The handler repeats handler-to-side outruns in a large circle around the sheep, dropping the dog at various intervals and/or when dog tries to cut in. The handler must be repositioned after each time the dog is stopped.

BEGINNING SQUARE FLANKS (MAINTAINING THE WORKING RADIUS)

"Square flanking" refers to the movement when the dog begins to swing around the sheep. Initial movement should be at a 90-degree angle or more in order to stay off the sheep and get around them while holding the original distance from which the dog started.

Square flanks are vital for quiet working of the stock, preventing splitting or scattering of the flock, and when penning. If the dog is continually coming in closer to the stock and is not able to maintain a working radius, he will cause excessive pressure on the stock. Controlling the distance from the sheep that the dog works will be useful in adapting to different types of sheep. Light sheep move very easily and will require a considerable distance between them and the dog to maintain control, while heavy sheep require a dog to work much closer

DIAGRAM 19 - The Sling-Shot Outrun. The dog is between handler and sheep, closer to the sheep. The handler is positioned slightly *toward* the side of the Outrun and is initially facing away from the sheep. The handler's torso is rotated toward the dog and crook is in hand closest to the dog, pointed behind the handler and slightly toward the dog. The handler calls the dog off the sheep, followed by directional command for the Outrun. As the dog goes by, the handler rotates to follow the path of dog, sweeping the crook along behind the dog.

without the flock bolting past the handler or "exploding" all over the field.

The dog should be asked to hold the radius when wearing the sheep in figure eights and serpentines. The following exercises are helpful in continuing to have the dog work at a distance from the sheep and maintain the working radius.

The most elementary exercise is set up with the handler between the sheep and the dog (see Diagram 20). You will direct your dog "Go Back" (see Chapter 4) and have him move directly away from the sheep until he reaches the distance *you* wish to place him from the

DIAGRAM 20 - Beginning Square Flanking—Maintaining Working Radius. Handler Between Dog and Sheep. The handler is positioned between sheep and dog, and directs dog to "Go Back." The stock dog should move directly away from the handler. The handler then swings the dog both to the right and left with appropriate directional commands, encouraging the dog to maintain the new radius established by the "Go Back" command. A handler may need to move toward the dog to encourage him to stay out.

sheep. Then have the dog lie down. Direct your dog to swing from one side to the other in arcs that are approximately 180 degrees in the clockwise or counterclockwise direction ("Come Bye" or "Away to Me"). As the dog reaches the point of the arc that would come past you, direct him to lie down and then go in the opposite direction, maintaining the original distance (radius) from the sheep. If he cuts in, step toward your dog, slap the crook and say "Get Out." Drive the dog back to the original radius and make him maintain that distance from the sheep!

Eventually, you will be able to have the dog work on his feet and change directions without lying down. But early in training, it helps to stop the dog before sending him in the other direction.

After the dog will perform satisfactorily with you between him and the sheep, move to the opposite side of the sheep (see Diagram 21). If the dog cuts in or does not maintain the radius, you may have to run toward the side of the sheep or through the sheep to chase him back out again.

DIAGRAM 21 - Beginning Square Flanking (continued). After the "Go Back" command is established, this exercise should be practiced with the handler on the other side of the sheep. A handler may still need to move toward dog to help maintain the newly established radius from the sheep.

FENCE-LINE PICKUPS

This exercise is used to teach the dog to go between the fence and the sheep, moving sheep away from the fence (see Diagram 22).

To set the stage, have the dog hold or wear sheep *to* you as you back up to a fence. For this example, we will be having the dog pick the sheep up off the fence by going in the "Come Bye" or clockwise direction. You should stop and drop the dog at a distance that will hold the sheep on the fence. Then walk through the sheep, call your dog to you and place him a little to the left of the sheep as you are facing them. You then walk to the other side (right) of the sheep until you are about the same distance from the sheep as your dog and parallel to your dog. Face your dog and say "Get Out, Come Bye." Just as when

It is important to teach the young dog to be comfortable in close situations, such as when going between the sheep and the fence. He may want to fly in and grip, or circle the sheep. Your "quiet power" while practicing this will communicate confidence to your dog. The sheep should move smoothly at a walk or trot as they come off the fence.

you were doing the "Get Out" exercise, "Get Out" is the primary command and the direction is secondary. If your dog starts to come in too fast, get excited or grip, quickly have him lie down. Then again say "Get Out," adding "Steady" if he needs to slow down. As soon as the dog comes in behind the sheep along the fence, have him lie down so as not to get excited and fly into the sheep. Having the dog lie down will help him regain composure from being uncomfortable with this tight situation. As the sheep move away from the fence, have him "Walk In" to move them to you. You will have to back up in order to give the sheep someplace to go. This exercise will help him gain confidence when seeing the sheep move off the fence without a lot of commotion.

Do this exercise several times in both directions, allowing the dog to bring the sheep to you. Then you can gradually lengthen the distance the dog has to go to pick the sheep up off the fence (see chapter 6). Eventually he will be able to leave from your side, kick out and pick them up off the fence. As with other exercises, practice

DIAGRAM 22 - Fence-Line Pickups. The Handler's back is to fence. With the dog on the far side of sheep, the handler then walks forward through the sheep and to one side of the dog. Swinging around to the side of sheep, the dog should go between the sheep and the fence; *not* through the middle of the sheep. The dog may be sent in either direction, depending on the angle of the handler's path. As the dog swings around the sheep, the handler rotates to watch the dog, then backs up, allowing the dog to move the sheep to the handler and giving the sheep some place to go.

the uncomfortable direction (your dog's weaker side) several times as much as the comfortable direction.

Possible Problems with Teaching Fence-Line Pickups and How to Handle Them

1. **The dog flies in and grips as he comes between the fence and the sheep.** This is likely the result of extreme discomfort in a tight situation and may be worsened when your dog is going in his nonpreferred direction. Be quick with your "Lie Down" command so that you can have the dog lie down before exploding into the sheep. You also might try starting this exercise with the sheep a short distance from the fence, but in subsequent exercises gradually placing the sheep closer to the fence as your dog gets more comfortable.

2. **The dog slips in between the sheep and the fence, but goes all the way to the opposite side of the sheep before lying down.** This may be a problem if the sheep do not readily

As soon as the dog comes in behind the sheep along the fence, have him lie down so as not to get excited and fly into the sheep. Lying down will help the dog regain composure from being uncomfortable with this tight situation.

As the sheep move away from the fence, have the dog "walk in" to move them to you. You will have to back up to give the sheep someplace to go. This will help the dog gain confidence seeing the sheep move off the fence without a lot of commotion.

move away from the fence as the dog comes around behind them. Use your body language by stepping *toward* the dog as he comes too far around; snap your crook on the ground, saying "Get Back out of that." When he is in the right place, lie him down and give praise, letting him then get up and move the sheep toward you. It is important to keep things quiet and collected during this exercise, to avoid creating tension for your dog.

Also, evaluate your timing. It may be that you are not giving the "Lie Down" command quickly or early enough to stop the dog. If your dog knows to hold the comfort zone, you should be able to stop him on the fence just by using your body (no "Lie Down" command) and having him balance on you.

3. **The dog comes in fast for the pickup instead of slow and easy.** Make sure you tell your dog "Steady." You may use "Steady" before or after the "Get Out" command to remind the dog to go slowly. If need be, remind your dog what "steady" means *while wearing*, so that he will steady in the fence-line situation as well.

CONTINUING THE "CALL IN"

Continue to do "Call Ins" several times during the lessons. You should be increasing the distance that the dog has to come in, varying the situations in which you ask him to come in to you. You should be able to do "Call Ins" when the dog is excited as well as calm.

Once your dog will obey "Call Ins" well from 20 to 30 feet away and look at you *when you ask*, reduce the frequency of practicing this command. If your dog is constantly looking at you and wanting to come in to you, that may create problems in itself!

Use the "Call In" as a barometer of obedience. It should be there when you ask for it, but not be practiced so frequently that it causes a dog to be distracted from working the stock.

INTRODUCING DRIVING

In the drive, the dog moves *sheep away* from the handler, *not toward* the handler (see Diagram 23, A and B). The drive should not

In the drive, the dog moves sheep away from the handler, *not* toward the handler.

be introduced until you are able to stop your dog reliably and until both you and your dog have a working idea of the flanking commands. A dog should know what the command "Walk In" means and should be doing "Call Ins" well. At this stage, Border Collies should be doing outruns of 100 to 150 yards. Other breeds should be doing shorter outruns in good form.

If your dog is a gathering dog with a lot of natural ability, the drive may be difficult for him at first because it goes against the natural

113

DIAGRAM 23A - Introducing the Drive. The Handler introduces the Drive following a Fetch by stopping the dog on the opposite side of the sheep. The handler swings the dog around the sheep (in either direction) to the rear of the handler, then stops the dog there. The handler then has the dog walk straight in toward the sheep, causing the sheep to move away from the handler. At first, the dog is asked to drive the sheep only a few steps before being called off and set up for an Outrun and Fetch and a repeat of the sequence.

tendency to gather. Your dog may think he is doing it all wrong when you first ask him to drive! For dogs with driving styles, this task may come much more easily.

Start with your dog on the long line. Have your dog do an outrun and bring the sheep to you. Once this has been done, flank him around to the opposite side of the sheep so that you are between dog and sheep, but close to the sheep. Call your dog in to you by saying "Walk In, come here." He should come in easily since you've already taught the "Call In." Then hold the long line and encourage your dog to walk on past you and toward the sheep. If the sheep start to bend around toward you, step out to that side so that your dog will be able to straighten them out.

114

DIAGRAM 23B - The Drive. Dog is moving sheep *away* from the handler and is located between the handler and the sheep. Handler, sheep and dog are all moving in the same direction.

Keep encouraging your dog to move toward the sheep with ''Walk In, good dog!'' *Remember, always keep the tone of your voice low, quiet and reassuring.* You may have to walk along with your dog, or even lead him in, at first. As soon as you can, *gradually begin to drop back and let your dog lead you*—first by a head, then to his shoulder, then a body length or the length of your line (with slack in it). The first time or two, you may only drive the sheep several feet or yards. Then have the dog lie down, call him off and send him on a short outrun. Then set your dog up and start the drive again.

For dogs with natural driving styles, such as the Corgi, this task may come much more easily.

Encourage the dog to walk on past you and toward the sheep. Having the dog wear the sheep past you during the fetch is often a good way to start the drive.

You may have to walk along with, or even lead in, your dog as he begins to learn to drive.

As soon as you can, gradually begin to drop back and let your dog lead you—first by a head, then to the shoulder, then a body length or the length of your line (with slack in it).

This time you may be able to drive the sheep 10 to 15 feet before the dog gets very anxious. If your dog gets anxious or does not "Steady" right away when you ask, stop and then call him off again. Take the dog back and let him do an outrun. If at all possible, *do not allow your dog to go directly from a drive into a gather.* Don't all of a sudden allow him to take off and swing around the sheep and bring them back to you! This can quickly become a bad habit! During beginning and intermediate driving training, *always* break up the drive and the gather by stopping your dog, calling him off and then sending him on the outrun.

As you work on this, you will gradually be able to drive a little farther. Aim to drive a little farther than your dog may want, but don't push it to the point that he will get in trouble!

Try to drop back and increase the distance between you and your dog as quickly as possible so that you are not a crutch to the dog. He needs to feel confident to drive the sheep without you being right there. *You cannot force confidence—you need to stay close enough to help your dog and keep things from falling apart.*

I want to caution you about doing too much flanking while driving at this stage. For one thing, your dog has never flanked with you behind him before and most likely will not understand what you want! In addition, if you start flanking too much, you may be starting a "push-

Try to drop back and increase the distance between you and your dog as quickly as possible so that you are not a crutch to the dog.

button dog'' that just waits for your commands to work. You should not get in a hurry, during driving, to have the dog do turns that require flanking. If a dog is driving well and the sheep are bearing in a large circle, just let them continue the turn! It is important that the dog learn continuity in driving before learning flanks.

Introducing Flanking While Driving

There are two main ways to teach flanking while driving—pushing the dog away from you (see Diagram 24) and pulling the dog toward you (see Diagram 25).

To push the dog away from you in a clockwise (''Come Bye'') direction, you should move to your right so that you are off balance in the direction that will result in clockwise movement by your dog. You should be walking parallel to and approximately opposite your dog and on his *right* side. To ask him to flank clockwise, say ''Come Bye.''

DIAGRAM 24 - Flanking While Driving—Dog Is Being Pushed Away from the Handler. The dog is driving sheep, with the handler walking approximately even with and parallel to the dog. The sheep are drifting away from the handler, who pushes the dog away by commanding "Away to Me." "Get Out" may be used with the directional command to encourage square flanking, or if the dog tries to cut in. As soon as the movement of the dog corrects the path of the sheep in the desired direction, the handler swings the dog back behind the sheep in order to continue the drive.

119

DIAGRAM 25 - Flanking While Driving—Pulling the Dog Toward the Handler. The stock dog is driving sheep, the handler approximately even with and parallel to the dog. Sheep are drifting toward the side where the handler is located. The dog is pulled toward handler by the command "Here, Come Bye." Pulling the dog toward the handler keeps the dog from cutting in while swinging around the sheep. As the path of the sheep is corrected by the movement of the dog, the handler swings the dog back behind the sheep to continue the drive.

Be ready to have him lie down quickly! When you say "Come Bye," he will be thinking, "I thought you'd never ask!" and want to swing all the way around the sheep and bring them back to you. Don't let that happen! If your dog tries to cut in, a "Get Out" can be added ("Get Out, Come Bye") to encourage the dog to keep flanks square.

To set the stage for pulling your dog toward you for a clockwise flank, you will be walking parallel and approximately even with your dog and on his *left* side. To get the dog to take the clockwise flank, say his name and "Here, Here, Come Bye." Using "Here" will break his intense concentration on the sheep and help a dog keep the flanks square as he takes the directional command. Be sure you see your dog turn and look at you a little in response to the "Here" before you give the "Come Bye" command. Again, be ready to stop the dog quickly so that he won't swing all the way around the sheep and bring them back to you. These directional terms can and should be used as needed, to keep the flock going in as straight a line as possible. Start dropping farther back letting the dog do the driving alone.

If the sheep start to split, have your dog lie down. Allow the sheep to drift ahead, allowing the dog to gain perspective. Then by telling the dog "Get Out" or "Here" (pushing the dog out or pulling him toward you), help the dog to put the sheep back together. If you had just allowed your dog to continue driving, he might not have seen this split, and would have kept on going without keeping the sheep from splitting. Or, worse yet, the dog may have gotten so confused by the developing split that he might fly in, try to gather one group of sheep or another or otherwise get into trouble while driving.

Possible Problems While Introducing Driving and How to Handle Them

Possible problems when introducing driving and flanking include:

1. **The dog does not want to "Walk In" past you.** Remember to be encouraging. If this is a gathering dog, driving will go against instincts and natural tendencies. If this is a timid or sensitive dog, he may not be sure that this is something you really want him to do! Be patient, walk with your dog and *help* him move the sheep at first, or for as long as it takes for him to gain confidence. *Remember, this is a partnership.*

2. **The dog swings around the sheep and brings them back to you when driving.** Use the long line! Have it short enough that you can stop your dog if he tries to swing around the sheep. Be ready to have him lie down quickly if he begins to get anxious. Make sure you are not asking him for too much too soon. Be satisfied with short successful drives of a few feet or yards in the beginning.

3. **The dog does not obey "Steady" or "Lie Down."** Make sure you have done your homework in the earlier stages of training. Go back and make sure your dog understands "Steady" while wearing and will slow down when you say it, *without* your aggressive body language and/or use of the crook. Be sure the dog will "Lie Down" in *both on-balance and off-balance* situations. Go back to the Daisy Wheel Pattern (refer back to Diagram 18) to re-establish your authority for off-balance stops.

   If you are sure your dog understands the commands in these situations, it is possible that you are asking too much too soon while driving, or that the dog is being blatantly disobedient.

If you back up and ask for slightly less, see if your dog will obey then. If so, stay at that level for this lesson and then try to increase the difficulty gradually over the next few lessons. If there is still disobedience, it is likely that your dog needs a good, stiff correction to remind him of his responsibilities. Remember, never correct with anger! Correct dispassionately to get your point across without creating damage.

4. **The dog does not pay attention when you say "Here" to pull him toward you for flanking.** Remind your dog what "Here" means during another exercise, such as the "Call In," and in conjunction with "That'll Do" when you are calling him either off the sheep or around you for Handler-to-Side or Sling-Shot Outruns. You may need to have hold of the long line when you say "Here" while driving, giving it a slight tug to get your dog's attention. Remember that you do *not* want the dog to come all the way to you when flanking while driving. You just want to break his intense concentration on the sheep and keep his flanks square.

5. **The dog wants to come all the way back to you or go around behind instead of staying between you and the sheep.** It is easy to see why your dog might think this was the thing to do! Up until this time, you have been calling the dog off and pulling him around you, and you have done all your flanking with you placed between dog and sheep or on the far side of the sheep.

   If your dog starts to come all the way back to you, quickly have him lie down and then walk him back in a little before giving the flank command again. Or back up, giving the dog more room between you and the sheep and giving a "hiss" (*"Shhh-h-h"*) to encourage your dog to get onto the sheep again. Some breeds of dogs that are very laid-back or very sensitive to the handler may take a long time to figure out what is wanted with driving and flanking while driving. Be patient and upbeat in your approach.

Driving Along the Fence

By this time your dog should be comfortable driving the sheep away from you and you should be able to stop and call him off easily. The dog should now be ready to drive the sheep along a fence. He

The placement of the fence on one side of your dog and you on the other (toward the center of the field) will minimize a dog's chances of swinging around the sheep.

should also be learning how to hold the comfort zone. Your dog needs to learn to check himself and slow down as the sheep speed up, and not to keep crowding them. This is something that most dogs have to be taught. Most often it is not a natural reaction.

As your dog is driving along the fence with the fence on the right side of the sheep (counterclockwise around the field), you should be walking approximately opposite your dog and about 50 feet away toward the inside of the field. The placement of the fence on your dog's right and you on the left toward the center of the field will

123

minimize the chances of a dog swinging around the sheep, since the fence blocks one side and you and the dog's desire to balance on you block the other.

You will now have the dog drive around the field. If the sheep want to run, there are two things you will want to practice:

1. Some of the time, if the dog is being pushy, have him lie down and let the sheep run a short distance. Unless they are headed all the way back to the barn, they will likely slow down and stop. Then walk your dog in to them slowly and steadily.
2. Other times, pull the dog around toward you and toward the front of the sheep just enough to keep them from running.

Your *timing and placement* of your dog *are critical* in doing this. You want to keep the sheep walking, but not have them run. In addition to developing *your* ability to read the sheep, this will help *your dog* learn to read an unequal pressure from the sheep and keep them walking, not running.

Driving Continuously in an Oval

Another exercise that is useful in driving is to pull the sheep off the fence and have your dog drive them in a large oval around you. As he drives down the long side of the oval, walk down the center of the field. At each end of the oval, stand still while your dog makes the turns. You will be able to stay in close contact without being a "crutch" to your dog. As far as your dog is concerned, he will be driving continuously. This will help a dog learn to drive as long as you wish. You may have to help in the corners a little by flanking him out. By doing this exercise you will be able to have your dog do a long drive without your losing contact.

As you continue, you will want to be sure the dog knows his directions while driving and maintains square flanks. There is another square-flanking exercise that you will want to do—having your dog maintain the working radius while moving between you and the sheep (refer back to Diagram 21). Set up with the dog between the sheep and yourself. Swing the dog in an arc around the sheep, to approximately 90 degrees from where you are standing, making sure that he stays out the same distance he started from the sheep (maintaining the radius of the circle). Lie him down at this point, then flank him back toward you and on around the sheep in the other direction, making sure the dog stays between you and the sheep. At the same time, tell and help your dog to stay out. Or if he starts to close in on the sheep, pull him toward you by saying "Here" with the proper flank command again, so he can understand what you want. At the same time you may need to say "Get Out" or "Stay Out." It is imperative that a dog learn to hold his radius while flanking on a drive. Sometimes it helps for the handler to move a little in the same direction as the flank as the dog comes by. Eventually, you will be able to stand still and have your dog swing in arcs first one way and then the other while between you and the sheep.

"GET OUT" WHEN YOUR DOG IS BETWEEN YOU AND THE SHEEP

In addition to directions, your dog will have to learn to "Get Out" when working between you and the sheep. To this point you have used "Get Out" to move the dog farther away from the sheep *and* you. Now he has to learn to get out and away from the sheep while you are on the outside looking in. To accomplish this, integrate the "Get Out" command with pulling your dog toward you and flanking him around the sheep ("Here, Here, Get Out, Come Bye"). The dog has to learn to kick out *away* from the sheep and *toward* you.

For breeds other than the Border Collie, all of these exercises are very important. It may require time to understand what you want and for your dog to keep working the sheep at greater and greater distances from you.

But by this stage, it is likely that you and your dog have quite a lot of "stick-to-it-iveness" built into your teamwork and approach to training. Persevere! It is possible for you and your dog to achieve all these things if you stick with it.

EXTENDED DRIVING WITH FLANKING

By now your dog should be driving well without your help, able to hold the comfort zone while driving and able to hold a pressure point to keep the sheep moving in a straight line when they would rather move in a different direction.

Let's say you are driving in a counterclockwise oval with you on the inside of the oval (to your dog's left) and approximately opposite your dog. To have your dog flank in a counterclockwise direction, say "Get Out, Away to Me." This is an extension of the "Get Out" exercise described previously. (Refer to Diagram 24.) To get your dog to flank in a clockwise direction, you will say "Here, Here, Come Bye." (Refer to Diagram 25.) *Make sure you practice the oval in both directions and practice both flanks* on the clockwise and counterclockwise ovals.

This exercise also is an extension of pushing your dog away and pulling your dog toward you while driving, adding the "Get Out" command.

Be aware that your dog's uncomfortable direction will resurface while flanking during driving exercises. Be sure to practice more in his uncomfortable direction to help balance him up. But it probably won't take as long to balance him up on his flanking while driving as it did when you were teaching directions and outruns.

MORE DIRECTIONAL COMMANDS AND OFF-BALANCE MOVEMENT

By this time, your dog should understand the directional commands. Be sure to practice in intense situations and when the dog is off balance. This gives your dog confidence in himself and in you and helps him realize that it is not always necessary to be in balance with you.

A good rule of thumb is to have your dog go in the *opposite* direction to that which he goes naturally. This establishes your control and helps your dog learn to handle control situations that could shake his confidence. Off-balance work also helps establish an essential bond and teamwork between you and your dog that would not be formed if your dog is allowed always to follow natural instincts and abilities that lead a dog to work on balance.

There are many opportunities to incorporate off-balance work in your daily training sessions. If the sheep are starting to drift in one direction or another, send your dog to gather them or flank them in the direction that is *not* the one he would chose on the basis of balance alone. If the dog is positioned to make it easiest to go in the clockwise direction, send him counterclockwise. Use opportunities to make your dog come toward and past you or those where you have him pull off of a heavy pressure point in order to flank.

126

DIAGRAM 26 - Off-Balance Work: Getting the Dog to Take Command. Continue the sudden commands and off-balance work. This should condition your dog to give an instant and automatic response to a flank command.

Possible Problems with Off-Balance Work and How to Handle Them

If the dog refuses to take direction in an off-balance or heavy-pressure situation, go back to the Daisy Wheel Pattern (refer back to Diagram 18) and re-establish control in that exercise. If he still refuses to go off balance, call your dog's name and say "Here," or give the dog a quick pull toward you, using the long line, diverting the dog's attention from the stock momentarily. This will break the intensity, helping the dog to feel free to move.

If your dog does not take a command to move off balance, another alternative is to walk up so that you are slightly in front of the dog, to the side you want your dog to go *from*. Then slap the ground sharply with your crook and tell him to go in the desired direction, escalating the command from a request to a reprimand (see Diagram 26).

These measures should solve the problem. If problems still exist, step back and try to analyze what is wrong. It may be that your timing is off or that you are not standing in a position that will encourage the dog to come on around you.

Most dogs, at this stage, will be ready to be set up beside the handler at the start of the outrun. When you start out setting your dog up beside you, you will be modifying the "Get Out" exercise and will be discontinuing the Sling-Shot Outrun.

6

Advanced Stages of Herding Training

"We are what we repeatedly do. Excellence, then, is not an act, but a habit."

Aristotle

OVERVIEW

By this time you and your dog should be well on your way to becoming a team. Both of you should be accustomed to working both light (easily moved) and heavy (harder to move) sheep in a variety of locations. This is invaluable in making a reliable and useful stock dog and in developing the handler's *and* dog's ability to work as a team.

The advanced stages of training involve some new exercises and tasks, but also require polishing and perfecting of many of the exercises and tasks with which you and your dog already are familiar. New tasks will include close contact work, penning and shedding or splitting.

PERFECTING THE OUTRUN/LIFT/FETCH

You should gradually be lengthening the outrun. Most dogs at this stage will be ready to be set up beside the handler at the start of the Outrun. When you start out setting your dog up beside you, you will be modifying the "Get Out" exercise (see chapter 4) and will be discontinuing the Sling-Shot Outrun. For example, if you are doing an outrun in the "Away to Me" or counterclockwise direction, you will have the dog on your right side and facing in the direction you want her to go. Your dog should be standing ("Stand, Stay"), ready to go at your command.

You will walk out so that you are on the left side of the dog and about 15 or 20 feet away. Then you will say "Get Out, Away to Me." That will help her kick out as she starts off on the Outrun. If your dog doesn't stay out, you will then head at an angle for the right side of the sheep so that you can get there quickly and blow the dog out and away from the sheep. This will make her maintain working radius while swinging around them.

While getting used to this setup, allow your dog to be closer to you at the start of the Outrun. Instead of saying "Get Out," you will be able to give the directional command or use a hiss or "*Sh-h-h-h*" sound to send her off.

Starting Your Dog on the Outrun

Sometimes a directional command will cause dogs who know how to square their flanks properly to go on *too much* of a square path for the Outrun. This is why some people prefer the "*Sh-h-h-h*" or hiss command to start the dog. It starts the dog off on a little more of an angle toward the sheep and keeps a dog from kicking out so much that you will lose points on the trial field.

Be careful, as your Outruns get longer, that the *path* of the Outrun does not deteriorate. There is a fine line between pushing your dog a little past the current level in order to improve, and pushing her faster and longer than you should. Be careful that your dog maintains an arc while passing around the sheep. Don't let her flatten the arc or cut in toward the sheep. By this time, if your sheep are used to being worked, they will often head for the handler before the dog has completed the arc of the outrun. This usually will start a dog cutting in at the top of the outrun and may start a bad habit. You may then need to have a friend with a dog hold the sheep for you so that you will be able to practice outruns correctly. Or you can use a release pen to hold the sheep when you are practicing outruns.

The release pen is used to hold sheep while doing outruns. It requires two people—one to work the dog and one to operate the pen. The sheep are loaded into the pen through the end gate. As the dog passes a predetermined point on the outrun, the pen operator pulls the rope to open the front swing gate, allowing the sheep to move out of the pen as the dog comes around behind them. The crawl space for the dog allows the dog to walk straight in toward the sheep to move the sheep out of the pen. It allows the dog to come in behind the sheep and move the sheep to the handler without deviating from a straight path.

The release pen can be used as a training tool or in trials to standardize the positioning and movement of the sheep for each dog. In trials the gate can be opened as the dog passes a predetermined point or a stake set in the ground. A word of caution, however: The release pen does have a tendency to draw the dog in at the top of the outrun; if you cannot keep your dog out at the top, you should not continue to use the release pen for training.

The Lift and Fetch

When at the top of the outrun, it is important that the dog develop the habit of coming in slowly and steadily to lift the sheep. If properly trained, this habit should persist for life! This is why it is important for dogs to learn to maintain their own comfort zone.

Earlier in training, you encouraged the habit of coming in slowly and steadily, by stopping your dog at the top of the outrun and then saying "Walk In." If you see the dog stop or slow down, you should let her walk in and you should not say anything. If your dog is coming in too fast, you may want to stop her, say "Steady" and then "Walk In" to lift the sheep.

As you increase the length of the Outrun, be careful that the dog does not push the sheep faster and faster while fetching them to you. This can become a habit very easily. You should constantly take care that this habit does not start. Your dog must learn to bring the sheep to you at a moderate speed. She must be taught to drop back as the sheep speed up, not to speed up as the sheep speed up. Don't let this habit go on—shut it down immediately! At this stage, don't send the dog on blind Fetches where you can't see what's happening on the fetch.

One "obedience thermometer" you can use to check your authority on the Outrun is your ability to bring the dog on around the sheep and head them (stop them) on the Fetch. If you have a Border Collie, you should be able to do at least a 150-yard outrun before you attempt this. With other breeds, you should be doing an outrun of a length that is competitive for trial work. After the dog picks the sheep up, give a flank command and bring her around in front of the sheep (see Diagram 27). If your dog will not do this, there is a hole in your authority. Dogs will not come on around without confidence in your handling and authority. They must believe that when you say to do something, you mean it!

I've never had a dog that would do this the first time asked. And probably, this wouldn't be the type of dog I'd like to have if she did! In order to teach coming on around the sheep on command, first you will want to practice asking your dog to flank on the outrun. She will probably take the flank command, come part of the way around and then reach a point so far off balance that she can hardly stand it, and will then want to fall back in behind the sheep.

DIAGRAM 27 - Square Flanking Continued: Bringing the Dog Around the Sheep. The dog is sent on an Outrun around the sheep. Instead of allowing the dog to complete the Lift and Fetch, the handler commands the dog to come around the circle, holding the working radius. A handler encourages the dog to come on around by stepping *toward* the dog (in this example, to the handler's right) and saying "Come Bye, Here" to bring the dog around and in. "Get Out" may be added to the command to remind the dog to maintain the radius of the circle.

So if you are going to flank your dog in the "Away to Me" direction, say "Away to Me." As you see her kick out and start around, you will run to your *left*, out to the side of the sheep. Then call and say, "That'll Do, Here, Here, Away to Me," encouraging the dog to come on around the sheep. Try to end up so your dog is *between* you and the sheep. Then have her drive the sheep away from you.

It is important that caution be exercised when bringing your dog around, as described above. Only do it until you can get it done. Don't practice it too much, or it may become a bad habit. If you do it too often, the dog may do it when you don't want her to! She may be fetching some sheep to you at a trial and you will ask her to flank because you need her to react quickly, and the dog may come clear around and shut the sheep down! This is *not* what you want to happen and it will certainly not make you look good! So, practice it until you can do it, but don't do it too often after that. Only do it once in a while to make sure you have complete control of your dog.

Encouraging Self-Sufficiency in Your Dog

It is important to allow the dog to think independently while bringing the sheep to you in a straight line. This requires decreasing the amount of verbal direction you supply and encouraging self-sufficiency in the dog that will be beneficial in tough situations. Have your dog bring the sheep to you over natural obstacles such as ditches, trees or creeks. Have her fetch the sheep with another dog in the path or with another dog or a group of sheep off to one side, exerting pressure that your dog will have to read in order to keep the sheep coming straight toward you.

Your judgment is important in decreasing the amount of verbal direction, since some verbal commands or support may still be needed in problematic situations. It is important to read your dog and know whether or not she needs help. An indication that help is needed is a dog who consistently gets into trouble, and the Outrun/Lift/Fetch is starting to deteriorate.

Possible Problems Perfecting the Outrun, Lift and Fetch and How to Handle Them

If the dog does not stop at the top of the longer outrun when asked to do so, set your sheep up about 75 or 100 yards away and put your running shoes on! If you place the sheep closer than that, it is likely that you will have enough control and the dog will not cheat. Therefore, have the sheep far enough away so that your dog will cheat on you, but not so far away that you can't run out there to them!

Send the dog from your side, then run up the field, straight toward the sheep. Your goal is to meet your dog as she comes around the back of the sheep. Run right through the sheep and blow the dog back out of there, scaring her. Your dog should think, "What in the world? How did you get here!?" and should be surprised!

Try to portray what I call "calculated anger." You want to convey to the dog that you are mad as a hornet, *but* this is a "calculated anger" since you do not want to do any real damage, as you might if you truly lost your temper. After your dog blows back out off the sheep, have her lie down. Leave her there and walk all the way back to where you started and have the dog bring the sheep to you slowly. If the sheep follow you back, that's all right—have her walk in slowly, *all* the way in, stopping your dog if necessary in order to get her walking in slowly.

Then set up again and do it again. You may have to run this same pattern four or five times in a row, but I guarantee that, in the end, your dog will stop at the top of the outrun when you say to do so.

ADVANCED FENCE-LINE PICKUPS

Fence-line pickups should continue to be practiced, increasing the distance the dog has to go (see Diagram 28). You will gradually be able to place yourself farther from both the sheep and the dog.

For example, to set the stage for a clockwise pickup you should stop your dog slightly to the left (the "Come Bye" side of the sheep) at the desired distance. You should be toward the right (or the "Away to Me" side) of the sheep and approximately the same distance away from the sheep as the dog is. This allows the sheep to move toward you as the dog moves them off the fence.

Gradually, you can increase the distance the dog has to go. Make sure that there is a *controlled* lift off the fence. Do not let the dog charge in behind the sheep, creating panic within the flock.

DIAGRAM 28 - Fence-Line Pickups from a Distance. The dog is stopped slightly to one side of the sheep at the desired distance from the fence. The handler is approximately the same distance away from the sheep and on the side opposite the dog. This allows the sheep to move *toward* the handler as the dog moves them off the fence. The dog may be stopped behind the sheep in order to maintain a controlled lift off the fence.

Possible Problems with Advanced Fence-Line Pickups and How to Handle Them

1. **The dog grips while bringing sheep off the fence.** It is likely that the dog has gotten into this habit because of being uncomfortable when first starting this exercise, the sheep didn't get out of the way and the dog was allowed to get excited. In order to cure this, you should get the dog doing some close-contact work. (See section ''Close-Contact Work'' in this chapter). Be sure you use a small area or fenced alley-way (approximately 12 feet by 16 feet). It is important that

this area be oblong and have square corners. This will help build your dog's confidence in her ability to get between the sheep and the fence without feeling the need to grip.

2. **The dog seems to be afraid to go between the sheep and the fence.** This problem requires the same approach as the problem with gripping discussed above. During this phase of training, be careful not to put the dog in with aggressive sheep— you must use sheep that will move away from the dog. Follow the suggestions in the section on close-contact work.

3. **The dog wants to "blow in" or move too fast.** This is also a sign of discomfort. This may be the result of having practiced fence-line pickups before you had a good down on the dog. Just like the two problems listed above, this one will require close-contact work to remedy the discomfort. Close-contact work will help this dog feel good and gain confidence. None of these problems will be cured by working on the fence-line pickups alone. But after doing close-contact work, when you come back to the fence-line pickups, you will find that most of your problems will have been resolved.

ADVANCED WORK WITH HERDING BREEDS

Breeds of herding dogs other than the Border Collie may require some more time and patience to master the longer outrun, lift and fetch. Some dogs may start off with less natural ability, so you may have to do more controlled work and more obedience work with them. This often does not give them a lot of confidence in themselves, so you will have to be confident *for them* at first. They have to learn to stick to the task in training so that you can accomplish what must be done.

All this takes time. You may have to repeat exercises often and frequently to get them to understand what you want and how you want it done. But at the same time, these dogs often are not intense enough to take repeated drilling in an area and you will constantly need to provide variety in what you are doing to keep them interested. By taking care of all the details and building on a good foundation, you should be able to take any breed of herding dog with instinct to work stock and make her into a useful herding dog. If you are committed to stick to it, you can get it done!

PENNING

The ability to pen stock is very useful and is a part of virtually every trial for stock dogs. To introduce penning, start with the Fence-line Penning exercise (see Diagram 29). You may have to work with some sheep that are not used to you and your dog, since the sheep you've been working may not move away from you fast enough when you bring the dog toward them.

To set the stage, back up to a fence with the sheep between you and the dog. Direct the dog to swing around the sheep toward you (dog is swinging off balance) so that the sheep bolt away from the dog. Then quickly command the dog to swing in the other direction to catch the sheep and bring them back to you. This should be repeated several times during a session until the dog anticipates what the sheep will do and will regroup them with minimal or no direction. This exercise teaches the dog to read the sheep and hold them to you while maintaining a proper comfort zone.

DIAGRAM 29 - Fence-Line Penning Exercise. This exercise encourages quick reactions by the dog while penning, as well as maintaining handler control. The handler backs up to the fence, with the sheep between the dog and the handler. The handler then directs the dog to swing around the sheep, causing them to *bolt away* from the dog. The handler then quickly commands the dog to swing in the other direction to catch the sheep and return them to the handler. This should be repeated until the dog can easily read the sheep and hold them to the handler while maintaining a proper comfort zone.

Once your dog is used to the Fence-line Penning exercise, she is ready to go to the Fence-Line-with-a-Gate Penning exercise (see Diagram 30). Start with the Fence-line Penning exercise along a fence in the area of the gate. Then open the gate slightly *toward* yourself, allowing one sheep at a time to go through.

After all the sheep have gone through, walk in to the entrance of the open gate and tell the dog "Lie Down," petting and praising her for a job well done. **Caution**: Do *not* let the dog fly through the gate, regroup the sheep and bring them back out without being told to do so! Instead, shut the gate and walk away, calling the dog off ("That'll Do"). This helps the dog realize that the job of penning has been completed. Then you can return and have your dog bring the sheep out of the pen and go on to some other exercise.

At this point your dog should understand what to do at the pen. She should be able to catch the sheep if they try to get away and know that you only want the *sheep* through the gate, and the dog should not go through the gate after them.

You have to set the stage repeatedly for a dog to learn these things. You may have to hold the gate closed and bring the dog in too close, so that the sheep will blow by. This creates an opportunity for dogs to learn to catch and regroup them, holding the working radius

DIAGRAM 30 - Fence-Line-with-a-Gate Penning Exercise. After swinging the dog several times using the Fence-Line Penning Exercise (Diagram 29), the gate should be opened slightly toward the handler, allowing one sheep at a time to go through. After all the sheep are penned, the dog should be stopped and dropped at the open gate. The handler should close the gate and walk away, calling the dog off the sheep with "That'll do" to help the dog realize the job has been completed. This prevents the dog from running after the sheep into the pen as well as preventing bringing them out of the pen before commanded to do so.

These two photographs demonstrate the Fence-Line Penning Exercise, which will teach the dog to respond quickly in holding the sheep to the handler. The dog swings around the sheep off balance, so that the sheep bolt away. Then the handler quickly commands the dog to swing in the other direction to catch the sheep and bring them back.

in order to keep a proper comfort zone. It is important that you force the sheep to try to get away from the pen and that you just don't have them walk into the pen because they know what to do! Your dog won't learn anything from this. Your dog will only learn by *doing*, so make sure you set up these situations correctly.

Next, you will need to practice penning in a pen that is set up in the open, away from fences, giving plenty of room for the dog to stay off the sheep without being against a fence (see Diagram 31).

Remember that penning is the result of a true partnership! The handler is only a small part of the whole scenario, with the dog controlling the majority of the circumference of the work zone, while the handler controls only a small portion of it. In trialing situations, you may help your dog by adjusting your body, but you cannot touch the sheep. You may, however, help your dog by getting down low to create a barrier and/or by extending your arm(s) and/or crook out to the side.

Stand at the gate of the pen, holding it open with one hand, with your crook in the other hand. As the dog brings the sheep toward the pen, try to head the sheep toward the hinge of the gate. This aligns them correctly for easier penning and minimizes the chances of losing them around to either side of the pen.

DIAGRAM 31 - Work Zones of the Dog and the Handler While Penning. The sheep are brought to the pen. Optimal alignment is usually when the sheep are headed directly toward the hinge of the gate.

When the sheep are at the mouth of the pen, this is the most critical time during penning, although you must be alert at all times! You should carefully read the sheep and try to figure out what *each* sheep is thinking of doing before it actually moves! This allows you enough time to move the dog appropriately to block the sheep's intentions. Often the only indication you will see is a slight turn of the head, raising of the head, or single step away from the other sheep. You should be ready to move your dog accordingly.

Moving the sheep into the pen requires great finesse. You should walk the dog in so that she slowly pushes the sheep into the pen, without creating excessive pressure or anxiety in the sheep that might cause them to blow back out of the mouth of the pen. Sometimes the dog gets in too close and creates so much anxiety in the sheep that they will be scared to turn their backs on the dog and will not walk into the pen. This is where a good "Go Back" is important to relieve the pressure and allow the sheep to relax. When they relax, they likely will move more willingly into the pen. Once the sheep are in the pen, close the gate most of the way. Bring the dog in to the gate and stop her at the mouth of the gate to prevent the sheep from coming back out. As before, give praise so that she understands that the job has been accomplished.

If your dog comes in too close, or gets progressively closer to the sheep with each flank command at the pen, you must get the dog to kick out, in order to relieve pressure. She should kick out *at least* far enough to double the distance between her and the sheep—and preferably a little bit more. As with other square flanking exercises, "Get Out" combined with the flanking command should help your dog to move away from the sheep.

But at the same time, you do not want a dog to "retreat" from the situation. If your dog tends to do this, you may have to call her in verbally or with a whistle each time you swing the dog to keep her at a standard distance.

SHEDDING OR SPLITTING

In most geographical regions, "shedding" is the term which refers to the task of splitting one sheep off from the others, having the dog hold it off from the other sheep.

"Splitting" the sheep generally involves separating more than

Stand at the gate of the pen, holding it open with one hand, with your crook in the other hand. As the dog brings the sheep toward the pen, try to head the sheep toward the hinge of the gate. This aligns them correctly for easier penning and minimizes the chances of losing them around to either side of the pen.

Often, at the pen, the only indication that a sheep is getting ready to move is a slight turn of the head, raising of the head or a single step away from the other sheep. You should be ready to move your dog accordingly.

142

It is important to understand what the sheep are planning, in order to have your dog in the proper place to prevent the sheep from escaping.

Bring the dog in to the gate and stop her at the mouth of the gate to prevent the sheep from coming back out. As before, give praise so that she understands that the job has been accomplished.

"Splitting" the sheep generally involves separating more than one sheep from the others, by calling the dog to you through the sheep. The "Call-In" exercise (below) discussed earlier will help to prepare the dog for this task.

one sheep from the others, by calling the dog to you through the sheep; the dog takes charge of holding these sheep away from the others. However, there is considerable variation in the specifics of these terms, depending on the area of the country.

When to Practice Shedding or Splitting

Try to do the shedding or splitting exercises at the beginning of a lesson, not at the end. The dog is more attuned to you at this time and is usually more willing and likely to come in to you quickly than when she is tired.

Introducing Shedding or Splitting Along the Fence

Most of the sheep used today for working young dogs are very people-oriented. Therefore, trying to have your dog start out shedding sheep in the middle of the field will prove virtually impossible! Introduce shedding by taking as many sheep as possible (the larger the number, the better!) to the side of the field and up against a fence (see Diagram 32). Work the dog back and forth slowly and quietly, just as you do for the fence-line penning exercise. Bring your dog back to a point opposite the center of the group and then walk her in one step at a time. If the sheep don't split on their own, you should push them apart, calling the dog in at the same time. Call the dog's name, saying "Come In, *Here*," emphasizing *here*. To encourage her to come into the small area between the sheep, you may have to call the dog and say "Here" repeatedly.

Once you start to call the dog in, make sure you follow through and bring her in to stand at your feet, while praising and petting. This should be done, regardless of whether the sheep regroup or stay split.

Then release the dog, regroup the sheep and reposition the dog opposite them. Repeat the "Call In," praising the dog until she will come in readily and quickly, causing the sheep to split apart. The quicker the dog comes in, the more likely the sheep are to split apart. Once the dog will do this, then it is time to indicate which sheep you wish the dog to split off and hold away from the rest.

Indicate the individual sheep or group of sheep you want to split off by turning toward that individual or group as the dog comes in, telling her "Walk In, *Here*," or "This One, *Here*," as you move slightly toward the group of sheep you want held. Repeat this command

To practice splitting along the fence, bring your dog back to a point opposite the center of the group and then walk him in one step at a time. If the sheep don't split on their own, you should push them apart, calling the dog in at the same time.

and give lots of encouragement. Initially, if your dog doesn't want to drive the one group away, work around to the opposite side of this group and allow her to wear those sheep to you and directly away from the other sheep. This will give the dog an idea of what you are after and help you stay in control of this situation. Once you have this group of sheep away from the others, try to get your dog to drive them a short distance to reinforce the split.

DIAGRAM 32 - Shedding or Splitting the Sheep. The sheep should be positioned along the fence. Larger numbers of sheep usually make this exercise easier, with the sheep to be held away from the others usually at the rear of the flock. The handler positions the dog opposite the sheep, and then may bend over and push the sheep apart. The dog may be brought in between the handler's hands to his/her feet with the command "Come In, Here" or "Walk In, Here." When learning to come in between the sheep, the dog is brought in to lie down at the handler's feet. As the dog learns to come between the sheep, the handler indicates the sheep to be held apart by rotating toward them as the dog comes in and telling the dog to "Walk In, Here." If the dog doesn't want to or is unable to drive them away from the rest of the flock, the handler should work around to the opposite side of the sheep to allow the dog to Wear those sheep directly away from the other sheep.

Splitting the Sheep in the Middle of the Field

After you have worked a few days on this and your dog has figured out what you want, it is time to move out into the middle of the field. This is more difficult than working on the fence-line! The sheep may be moving away from your dog as she moves in, and she needs to learn to come in quickly enough and far enough to cause them to split. If your dog comes in slowly, the sheep may be able to regroup and are not as likely to stay split apart.

If the sheep are difficult to separate, it is often helpful for you to try to push the sheep slowly toward the dog; usually this will cause the group of sheep to break apart slightly.

When splitting in the middle of the field, the dog needs to learn to come in quickly enough and far enough to cause them to split. If the dog comes in slowly, the sheep may be able to regroup and are not as likely to stay split apart.

Shedding Single Sheep

Don't be in too much of a hurry to shed single sheep; begin by splitting off at least two or more sheep for a while. Your dog must learn how to work with the unique pressures of working a few sheep away from another group of sheep to which they may desperately want to return. This is a very different kind of pressure than she has likely worked with before. Your dog must learn to stay back off the sheep and give herself the distance and time necessary to react to their movements. Dogs must be able to flank first one way and then the other to keep these sheep away from the others. If you get your dog in over her head too soon by splitting off a single sheep, she may develop a habit of gripping and/or coming in too tight.

Holding a Single Sheep Against the Fence

One of the things that is helpful, when you do get to the stage of cutting off singles, is to let your dog hold the single sheep against the fence while the remainder of the sheep are in the middle of the field. Holding the single sheep against the fence enables your dog to learn to work the very hard pressures exerted by this sheep that is wanting to get back to the others. The position of the one sheep on the fence keeps that sheep from cutting away and running wide to get back to the group. Have your dog hold this single sheep on the fence for a while, and then call the dog off and let the sheep return to the group.

This helps teach your dog not to overreact when dealing with extreme pressures. It is not unlike the overreaction of the novice driver when trying to steer around corners. At first he may turn too far, then overcompensate in the other direction, followed by the need to turn back again to straighten things out, creating even more trouble! Your dog has the same tendencies when learning to deal with extreme pressures, and in the process of overcompensating, may get "beat" by the sheep so that it can escape!

By moving along gradually, you can help your dog learn not to overreact. She will learn to stay off the sheep and not to come in and grip to shut things down.

Of course, in a trial, the judge will not have you hold the single sheep apart for very long. But if you train only for trials you will miss the opportunity to have a useful, well-rounded stock dog, and you will end up with one who has less than a proper, well-rounded education.

Holding a single sheep against the fence enables your dog to learn to work the very hard pressures exerted by this sheep that wants to get back to the others.

Additional Considerations for Shedding and Splitting

Remember to practice having your dog hold groups of sheep on each side of you. Don't always pick the group to your right. Dogs have to be balanced in this exercise, just as you developed her in circling, outruns and driving work.

Don't waste a lot of time out in the middle of the field with a young dog. If you just can't get the sheep to split, move to the fence. Don't let it turn into such a frustrating situation that neither you nor your dog learns something positive from it!

Possible Problems with Shedding or Splitting and How to Handle Them

1. **The dog doesn't seem to understand what to do.** This can be an extremely frustrating exercise for both you and your dog. Be careful not to allow your frustration to be communicated, since your dog is probably already uncomfortable about causing the sheep to split. It may take several sessions before your dog really catches on to what you are after. Stay cool!
2. **You can't get dog to focus on the group of sheep you want.** Try to get down low and stay close, holding your dog lightly by the collar if needed. Get her attention by saying ''Here,

After the dog has become comfortable with shedding off a few sheep and with working a single sheep along the fence, you will be ready to practice shedding a single sheep from the group.

Here, *these* sheep'' or ''This One, This One, *Here, Here*.'' Working yourself around so that the dog can wear this group to you for a short distance before you have her drive may help focus the dog's attention on the correct group. It may be very difficult for dogs with a strong desire to gather the sheep when they see another group of sheep nearby! By this stage in your training, your dog should have enough confidence in you and you should have enough authority over and understanding of your dog to help her learn and understand what you want done.

THE ''LOOK BACK''

The ''Look Back'' command is used to send your dog farther back to pick up a single sheep or group of sheep that she did not see or was not capable of seeing because of a position low to the ground (see Diagram 33). You may be able to see the sheep while your dog does not because of your height or a particular vantage point, especially in hilly or broken terrain. Usually the command or whistle ''Look Back'' is followed by a directional command to help place the dog in the correct position to find those sheep.

151

DIAGRAM 33 - The Look Back. The dog is stopped between two groups of sheep. The handler tells the dog to "Look Back," indicating that the dog should swing back and pick up the group of sheep behind the dog. A directional command may be used to tell the dog which way to swing to pick these sheep up. The "Look Back" command is used when there are additional sheep that the dog has not seen or is not able to see. When first teaching this command, the handler may need to walk toward the group of sheep that need to be picked up, helping and encouraging the dog.

Usually the "Look Back" is easily understood by the dog because it is a modification of the "Go Back" that has already been learned. Usually, many opportunities to teach the "Look Back" occur during your everyday training.

Importance of the "Look Back"

This command is extremely useful and beneficial in training. You will be able to use it whenever some of the sheep split off. It also is useful when working in the barn and your dog does not see a lamb lurking in the corner. Some dogs, particularly when they are young, do not like working small lambs and will go right by them. The "Look Back" will remind them to go back and collect the lambs, too.

Teaching the "Look Back"

If you have several sheep that have split off from the others so that you have two separate groups, have your dog bring the first group to you. Then step in between the dog and the sheep and tell her "Look Back." Keep walking toward the dog and the other group of sheep, repeating "Look Back." If your dog wants to collect the sheep that were just brought to you, have her lie down and then say "*Here*, Look Back." Keep walking toward the other group of sheep and repeating "Look Back," keeping the dog between you and the group of sheep

152

that you are after, until you see your dog spot those sheep. As soon as you see the dog recognize the other group of sheep, give a directional command to swing one way or the other around them. Let the dog bring those sheep to you.

Then, if you are far enough away and the first group of sheep have not followed you back, swing your dog around the sheep she has just brought to you and say "Look Back" for the first group. That way *you create two opportunities to practice the "Look Back" in one situation!*

CLOSE-CONTACT WORK

Close-contact work refers to having your dog work very close to the sheep in tight situations and enclosures. Close-contact work is important for moving sheep out of stalls, pens or trucks. It is important in developing your dog's confidence in her ability to work sheep in close quarters and in becoming comfortable in a variety of situations. Most dogs are not initially comfortable in a close environment. It is up to *you* to *teach* your dog to be comfortable in an uncomfortable environment.

To teach your dog close-contact work, you will need an enclosure

Close-contact work is important for developing confidence in all dogs, as well as for helping dogs learn that they can move sheep without gripping or without gripping harshly.

or barn aisleway that is approximately 12 feet by 16 to 24 feet with square corners. This enclosure should contain as many sheep as possible (usually thirty to forty). The sheep should be able to move away from your dog, but not easily.

Teaching Your Dog to Do Close-Contact Work

Mental Preparation

Before you even *think* about doing close-contact work, put your temper in your back pocket. You want to have a soothing effect on your dog. *You cannot afford to shout, get mad or lose your temper. You must project quiet confidence* at this time since this is what you want to instill in your dog.

Procedure

Start with your dog on a 5-foot-to-6-foot leash or line. Take her into the enclosure and start moving in the direction that your dog likes the best. Let's assume that the ''Away to Me'' side is your dog's most comfortable side. You will ease down the ''Away to Me'' side of the enclosure, staying between your dog and the sheep, holding the line in your right hand. You will be repeating ''Away to Me, Steady now, good dog'' to your dog as you go along. Your dog will probably be very anxious at this point, so you will need to continue to be reassuring her as you ease along.

If possible, try to keep your dog a little ahead of you—even if it is only half a body length. If not, try to coax your dog along, without pulling, staying between the dog and the sheep, leaving only enough room for your dog to stay against the wall or fence.

Then help your dog start to peel the sheep away from the wall, one by one. Every time one breaks away, your dog may want to grab it. Quietly caution with ''Ah-ah, none of that, Steady now, Away to Me, Away to Me.'' Every time your dog gets anxious, steady her both verbally and with a little check on the leash. Keep just enough slack in the line so that your dog can't fly in and create havoc, but do not hold the line tight. A taut leash tends to excite the dog, and will likely cause a grip.

If you have a really aggressive ewe, you can help your dog by pushing the ewe out of the way during your dog's early lessons. If you have a ewe that wants to face and challenge just a little but not go after the dog, just hiss the dog in for encouragement. Sometimes I get down

154

low and put my hands by the sheep's hocks, showing the dog just where to bite softly. Be careful not to overreact if he wants to grip. Keep your voice low to caution and correct her.

It will help if you try to work down low. Keep your hands down by the hocks of the sheep, if they are facing away from you. By doing this, you can help your dog get up close, maybe nip at their hocks just a little, and get her nose pushed in between the sheep and the wall. It doesn't matter if it takes five minutes or ten minutes to ease along and get the sheep to peel out of the corner. Once they move out of the corner, let your dog go around behind them. Have her lie down and then say what a good dog she is! Don't let her get up. Praise will help your dog understand just what she did and how great it was!

Now do the same thing to the "Come Bye" side. You will keep the line in your left hand and stay between your dog and the sheep. Quietly talk to your dog the same way in this direction, saying "Come Bye, Steady now, Come Bye," gently warning and checking her if she wants to grip or fly in.

As you continue to work on this, you will begin to see that your dog is becoming more confident and learning to use Quiet Power, not just flash-in-the-pan quickness.

You will want to have your dog move from one end of the aisle to the other five or six times during the first lesson on close-contact work. Usually I recommend doing close-contact work at the end of a regular lesson, after the dog has settled down and had the opportunity to work.

Keep working close to and with your dog until you feel that she is able to follow directions and move in to move the sheep off in a nice, orderly, quiet manner. Then you will be ready to start backing up and having your dog work more independently. Eventually you will be able to stay at one end of the small area and have your dog work quietly along to the far end.

When you can, let your dog figure out how to get around the sheep. If she wants to go under the sheep, between their legs or between the sheep and the wall, let her do it! If she wants to nibble at the hocks a little, that is fine. As long as your dog is not getting too aggressive, let her do it. This builds a dog's self confidence and confidence in you as a supportive partner, in what is initially a very strenuous and stressful situation. After your dog learns to do close-contact work, both of you will really enjoy being able to work stock in tight situations, but it may be very hard for your dog at first!

Remember to be quick with the "Lie Down" command when

your dog gets to the far end of the enclosure, because the natural tendency will be to "head" the sheep or stop them from moving. Every time a sheep wants to fly by, your dog may want to turn that sheep around to keep it from getting away. In such close quarters things happen so fast that the natural reflex will be to try to stop the action. It is important to be able to tell your dog "Lie Down" and have her honor this command as the sheep start to move. This will help the dog understand that you *want* the sheep to go to the other end of the pen or enclosure and that you *want* your dog to let this happen.

Usually, after three or four days of this kind of quiet work, your dog should be able to move the sheep while you stay at one end of the enclosure. But if she doesn't progress this rapidly, keep incorporating this kind of work into your training routine.

Importance of Close-Contact Work

Close-contact work is important for developing confidence in all dogs, as well as for helping dogs learn that they can move sheep without gripping or without gripping harshly.

It is important that you not let your dog grip harshly while introducing close-contact work. If you work just as described above and keep your voice low and your dog controlled, this work will translate into a lesser bite or grip than she has felt it necessary to use previously. Your dog will learn to use Quiet Power to move the sheep without gripping severely. It is a sophisticated way to take aggressive gripping out of a dog without any crash and thrash on her part or yours!

Increasing Control with Close-Contact Work

Once your dog is able to go from one end of the enclosure to the other, start your dog down one side and then have her lie down about one-fifth or one-fourth of the way along the side. This is extremely useful in moving sheep off of a truck! The sheep passed by the dog will start to move out the door. The remaining sheep, because of the dog's position, will only come by in small bunches. This prevents crowding and injuries to the sheep that are likely to occur if she was sent at once all the way to the back of the sheep.

It may be very difficult for a young dog to stay there and watch the sheep come by. But the dog will eventually see that it is working; the truck is being unloaded, and she can trust you and you can trust her!

156

Also, you will want to practice having your dog work to the end of the enclosure and then back up to the front of the enclosure (where you are) and push the sheep back to where they started. When your dog and you can do this, you are well on your way to having a well-trained, confident dog!

ADVANCED DIRECTIONAL COMMANDS AND OFF-BALANCE WORK

You will want to continue to refine your use of directional commands and your dog's responses in off-balance as well as on-balance situations. Now is the time in your training that your dog should take your directional commands solely because you ask. She must learn to do what you ask, when you ask. This is not a democracy; the dog does not have a vote in the decision!

In addition to situations that have been introduced in earlier chapters, you will want to make sure that your dog will obey off-balance directional commands while driving. If she is driving and holding a heavy pressure zone, you should be able to pull her off that heavy pressure zone.

For example, if your dog is driving and there is a heavy pressure zone to your right (on the "Away to Me" side) you will want to ask your dog "Come Bye." She will have to release this heavy pressure zone and come on around in the clockwise direction. Some dogs will come partway around and then fall back to the other side when the pressure becomes overwhelming to them. Work on this gradually so that your dog will not lose any natural ability to read pressures. But at the same time, enforce your authority. This will be an "obedience barometer" for you, along with the earlier exercise of bringing your dog on around the sheep on the fetch (refer back to Diagram 27).

Both of these obedience barometers will be helpful in determining if your dog has the confidence in you *and* the obedience necessary to perform successfully in trial situations.

Sometimes in trials, you will see your dog moving the sheep toward a gate, but because the pressure is so heavy and she is holding it so tightly, you see that the sheep are going to miss the gate. You must be able to get your dog to release this pressure when you say to do so in order to have the sheep pass *through* the gate.

WHISTLE WORK

Practicing Whistles Without Your Dog

Before trying to introduce the whistle to your dog, it is important that you practice using the whistle *without* the dog! You should consistently be able to produce whistles you have chosen to use for "Lie Down" (stop), "That'll Do," "Come Bye," "Away to Me" and "Steady." Many people also like to use a whistle for "Look Back."

Integrating Whistles with Verbal Commands

To teach the whistle commands, integrate them with the verbal commands your dog already knows. Say the verbal command, use the whistle and then repeat the verbal command. Most dogs pick up on whistles quickly, often preferring and responding better to them than to verbal commands.

The "Art" of Using Whistle Commands

As you become more accomplished with the whistle and your dog has learned the basic whistle commands, you may start using variations to bring her in or push her out, speed up or slow down. These subtle variations are accomplished with continued practice, starting with accompanying verbal commands.

Quick, sharp whistles tend to bring your dog in closer to the sheep; it is helpful to use longer, drawn-out whistles for the flanking commands so that she will stay out wide. Likewise, the "Steady" whistle should be long and drawn out instead of quick and sharp.

Listening to an experienced handler using a whistle is like listening to a conversation between the handler and the dog; the minor variations and changes in whistling can communicate as much or more to the dog as verbal commands.

158

7

Working Personality Types in Herding Dogs

"The secret of education lies in respecting the pupil."
Ralph Waldo Emerson

OVERVIEW

Seven basic working personality types may be identified in herding dogs. The personality profiles associated with each working personality type will be presented, along with strategies for working with each personality type and specific training techniques that may be needed to bring out the best in each type of dog.

Most dogs are a composite of several working personality types and may exhibit them to varying degrees. The personality types your dog displays may, in some cases, change with age, training and maturity. In other dogs, the personality type may play a major role in the dog's reaction and in your approach to training throughout your dog's life. In addition, there are several personality *traits*, separate and distinct from the personality *types*, that will influence your approach to your dog. These will be discussed for each personality type.

The basic personality types represent different extremes with regard to self-esteem, sensitivity to the handler and talent, enthusiasm and intensity for working stock. The basic personality *types* are

1. the talented dog;
2. the less-talented dog;
3. the hard dog;
4. the dog with low self-esteem;
5. the excessively pressure-sensitive dog;
6. the laid-back dog; and
7. the intense or keen dog.

Separate personality *traits* that will be considered include: the degree of aggressiveness with which your dog approaches the stock; your dog's degree of sensitivity to your authority; your dog's degree of sensitivity to pressure or to the actions of the stock.

THE TALENTED DOG

Characteristics of the Talented Dog

The talented or capable dog has a tremendous amount of instinct to work independently. This dog is very sensitive to pressure, without being excessively sensitive, and has a natural ability to read the sheep. He has a natural tendency to stay off the sheep and may naturally hold a distance from them when wearing. He seldom grips because of a natural tendency to stay off the sheep, but may sometimes "hit" the sheep from behind if he becomes bored with wearing during the early stages of training. Following this kind of hit, usually the dog will immediately kick off the sheep and put them all back together.

This dog may naturally stop when he reaches a balance point. He is usually extremely confident and self-assured and tends to be a "clean" dog, meaning that he naturally wants to keep the sheep together. The talented dog will usually start working on the handler, not just on the sheep, much more quickly than some of the other types of dogs.

Basis for the Behavior of the Talented Dog

This dog's behavior is a result of extreme confidence and natural ability. From the time this dog walks onto the field as a puppy, he may think he has everything all figured out and that the handler is just along

These two photographs demonstrate the talent of a four-month-old pup who is already able to bring a single sheep back to the flock. While this pup is too young to begin a training program, he has enough natural ability to be able to gather the sheep.

for the ride. As far as this dog is concerned, he has no need for you, the handler, to be out there at all!

This is an easy dog to work with in some respects because he naturally does many things right. However, this may be difficult to work with in other respects because of the dog's confidence in his own ability. Although the talented dog naturally knows a great deal, he *thinks* he knows it all already!

Working with the Talented Dog

Even a talented or capable dog can be turned off if you come down too hard at first. You will need to be patient in establishing command over instinct and getting this type of dog to trust your decisions and commands. This may be very difficult in situations in which the dog thinks the sheep are getting away. This type of dog will want very much to bring them back and may not easily understand that you want him only to do it when *you ask*.

Because this dog tends to respond to situations *naturally*, it is a challenge to set up situations that will enable you to effectively teach the necessary commands or terminology.

It is important to have the dog learn the terminology quite early in training. If you are not careful, you will find that you can go out and work in circles, figure eights and serpentines without really saying a word. Basically, the dog has learned to follow and hold sheep to you, but not much else! Therefore, you consciously have to set up learning situations, and to use the terminology necessary to establish command over instinct. You should always strive to preserve a good attitude and allow this dog to use natural instinct and ability, while establishing *yourself* as a necessary, useful member and head of the team.

Training Exercises for the Talented Dog

The talented dog will probably hold his distance off the sheep properly, so you will not have to do a lot of training to get him to do this. The problem with a dog that does this *naturally* is that you do not have a chance to teach the dog what "Get Out" means. Therefore, when you get in a tight situation, you do not have a command to make the dog get away from the sheep. You will have to set the stage to force the dog in too tight so that you can blow him out and teach what "Get Out" means.

You also may find that, by the second or third lesson, when you stop, the dog is going to stop and hold his distance from the sheep automatically. But how are you going to *teach* this dog to stop if he stops naturally and on his own? Again, you will have to set the stage

The young pup with natural talent is also comfortable with working a larger flock and has a natural tendency to stay off the sheep.

so that you can teach the stop command. You may have to call the dog to come in tighter than he should and then have the dog lie down.

While you are backing up and the dog is holding the proper distance, make him lie down and stay there until you get a fairly good distance away. Then you can say to "Walk In." This probably is the only way you will be able to teach the command "Walk In" as well, since he naturally knows to follow the sheep.

Make sure that your work with the talented or capable dog progresses *through all of the exercises* outlined in prior chapters for general training. Be sure that the dog is "balanced up on his sides" and able to go in both directions equally well and that you do not neglect any areas.

Remember that each dog is an individual and that even a talented dog will find some exercises harder to master than others. Do not ask the dog to do too much too soon and risk damaging a good attitude or establishing bad habits.

THE LESS-TALENTED DOG

Characteristics of the Less-Talented Dog

The characteristics of this type of dog will vary according to the breed of herding dog you are working. In general, the less-talented dog is deficient in varying degrees in the ability to read the stock and sense what the stock is going to do before they do it. This kind of dog may be *unable* to hold sheep against heavy pressure naturally or may not know how to balance or hold a balance point naturally. The less-talented dog may not know how to read the sheep and react appropriately, should they do something unexpected or want to run.

When considering the Border Collie, the dog of this personality type may have a very strong desire to work the stock, but is not able to be as delicate as a dog with more talent. This dog may overreact and overcompensate a lot of the time, even with training and experience. "Flopping" back and forth (see Chapter 4) in an older dog may be a sign that the dog is not able to read pressure well. A young dog of any personality type may "flop" as a result of immaturity and inexperience. But persistence of this tendency in an older dog may indicate a lack of talent.

Basis for the Behavior of the Less-Talented Dog

The herding behavior of this type of dog is based on lack of natural ability. Although he may have the instinct and desire to work, the natural ability to work is not high. This does not necessarily mean you should not work with this dog, but you should be aware that a lot of obedience will be required to compensate for the lack of natural ability. This means that the dog will need more "push-button" work, in which he relies on your commands to help him work the stock efficiently and effectively.

Working with the Less-Talented Dog

Working with the less-talented dog will require a lot of patience and good handling. Because you cannot rely on the dog to read the stock, you must become expert in this area. You must anticipate the behavior of the stock so that you have the time to tell your dog where and when to go and how to do things!

There will be times when your dog will not be able to handle things well, and he may let you down because of not being able to play at a high-level role in the partnership. Your goal will be understanding the level of talent that your dog possesses and helping develop whatever talent is present, should you decide to work with him.

If your dog is very aggressive, it may create a number of training problems for you. Because the less-talented dog tends to work very close to the sheep, this may contribute to triggering the kill mechanism and result in harsh gripping. Because this dog does not have a high degree of ability in balancing, during early training it may be difficult to get him backed off the sheep, to change directions and/or to stop.

It is of paramount importance that you be able to stop the dog and have him work off or away from the sheep and be equally comfortable going either direction, in order to train him and to obtain the degree of control that you will need in order to get the job done.

If you have a less-talented dog that is also very sensitive to your authority or has low self-esteem (see subsequent section ''The Dog with Low Self-Esteem)'', you will need to be very careful in establishing obedience and authority so that you do not turn this dog off from working stock. Because of a lack of natural ability, some of these dogs also may seem very laid-back (unenthusiastic) and may be easily distracted or discouraged from working. With these dogs you will have to be very upbeat and enthusiastic in your training.

With some breeds, you will need to be very careful in establishing obedience and authority so that you do not turn this dog off from working the stock. Because of the lack of natural ability, some dogs may be easily distracted or discouraged from working. With these dogs you will have to be very upbeat and enthusiastic in training.

It is important that you and your dog develop a lot of "stick-to-it-iveness" in your training. As long as you both enjoy training and you are satisfied with the progress being made toward maximizing whatever degree of talent that *is* present, I would encourage you to continue training and to have fun.

Training Exercises for the Less-Talented Dog

Dogs of this type may require more repetition of the training exercises, and may take longer to learn and understand what is wanted than do more talented dogs. But the general training program will be the same as that outlined in the text. In some areas, your dog may never have the ability to do the advanced exercises or exercises and tasks that require him to work independently.

THE HARD DOG

Characteristics of the Hard Dog

The hard dog is usually a very dominant individual. He feels the need to dominate other dogs to the point of being very aggressive toward them. Unless you are a very strong handler, both mentally and physically, this dog may dominate you as well! This personality type is at the one extreme of the spectrum, with little natural tendency to be sensitive to the authority of the handler. The dog with low self-esteem is at the opposite end of the spectrum. Ideally, you would like a dog that falls midway between these two types.

Many hard dogs have love for their owners, but not respect for them. In order to train your dog for herding, *both love and respect* for the handler must be present! It is very difficult for some people to handle this type of dog because of the constant battle of wills between handler and dog.

This is typically not a very powerful dog, even though he may be very aggressive. This type of dog tends to operate on the principle of "crash and thrash," and will take cheap shots and grip at any opportunity.

I have found that this type of dog seldom exhibits much talent. It may be that the talent is there, but the hard dog is *so* hard, aggressive and pushy that you have to impose a lot of control. The degree of control may be so high that you end up with a "push-button dog" in

You continually will have to take charge of handling the hard dog, as well as convincing that kind of dog to give you this level of control. If you just stand there, as the hard dog would prefer, it is guaranteed that your dog will not behave appropriately and will grip those sheep! It is important to get the dog widened out as early as possible in training.

which the talent has not surfaced or is hard to recognize! I have trained dogs in which I thought this was the case: On the rare occasion when they were not trying to push over the top of me, I could see a lot of talent in the way they worked. But it was never possible to get them to show this talent consistently, since the hardness would always reappear and the natural ability disappear.

Basis for the Behavior of the Hard Dog

The hard dog's behavior is based on a need to dominate and the tendency to continually test, dominate and control any situation. This basic personality will be a factor with which you will have to contend throughout the dog's life.

Working with the Hard Dog

If you do not have a genuine affection for your dog and if you are not willing to battle continually for dominance over the dog, I would recommend selling this dog or doing something other than herding. It is possible that he may be a decent farm dog for use on cattle, but it is unlikely that this will make a good trial dog.

Be sure that you correctly identify your dog's personality type and do not confuse a hard dog with one that just has a *touch* of hardness, resulting in him being pushy. The pushy dog may have a lot of heart and drive that may make him a champion if he also is talented. If you are not sure as to whether your lack of control is the result of extreme hardness in your dog's personality or is a problem with your training and handling, have your dog evaluated by a knowledgeable and experienced trainer who can advise and help you.

To try to avoid getting a dog of this type in the first place, always watch the parents work stock, and talk to people knowledgeable about the parents' tendencies and training. If the parents tend to push the handler around, it may be wise to stay clear of that line of breeding, particularly if you are a novice handler.

The hard dog may be a totally different dog around the house or kennel and may be agreeable, meek and mild. But when he gets on stock and the instinct comes into play, this dog may turn from Dr. Jekyll into Mr. Hyde.

It is important that you have a good "Lie Down" on the hard dog. The hard dog is typically difficult to stop and will push you to see what he can get away with most of the time. As I said, he is going to want to crash and thrash and is prone to take cheap shots, grabbing a flank on the way by the sheep. He may resemble the excessively pressure-sensitive dog in this respect, but the grip is the result of *more* than discomfort—he just wants to come in and take hold of something! You may have a variation of the hard dog with a concurrent tendency to be excessively pressure-sensitive. This makes your job even harder!

When you first start with your dog, you may not realize or recognize that you have a hard dog. The only sign that you may see at the initial exposure may be the tendency to grip harshly. However, as you continue with training, you will find that he will test you every day!

You continually will have to take charge of handling the hard dog, as well as convincing him to give you this level of control. If you just stand there, as the hard dog would prefer, it is guaranteed that your dog will not behave appropriately—and will grip those sheep!

This dog may work best on cattle, since they may require quite a bit of aggression and boldness. He will not be able to damage cows as easily as sheep. In addition, the cows may be able to teach him to have some respect for stock, since they are capable of doing some damage themselves. However, even with cattle, be careful if you have dairy cows that you do not want rushed or harassed, since the dog may be *very* forceful.

I prefer not to have a hard dog for myself since I do not want to continually fight this type of personality. And I would advise you against continuing to work with such a dog since there are plenty of dogs without extremely hard personalities that will make your herding experiences more fun and enjoyable!

THE DOG WITH LOW SELF-ESTEEM

Characteristics of the Dog with Low Self-Esteem

The dog with low self-esteem is very anxious when working. He may be easily shut down or turned off from working sheep if hit or walked on by a sheep in the early stages of training. He is sensitive to any overt or covert expressions of displeasure and/or lack of approval by the handler. This dog likes order and predictability in life and work.

He may not be very outgoing when meeting people and may be intimidated by situations in which there is a lot of noise and confusion.

He may tend to lie down when you pet him and may avoid making eye contact.

Some people may call this type of dog a "shy" dog. But he is not really shy. There is a difference between the shy dog and the dog with low self-esteem. Anything new bothers the shy dog. He quickly reaches the limits of any ability to cope with the environment and may react by fleeing or freezing. One manifestation of an extremely shy dog is the "fear biter." This dog resorts to biting when he cannot cope with the environment. Because his inability to cope may occur in many situations, this dog's actions may be extremely unpredictable—you may get bitten when you go to put the leash on him and/or when you go to take the leash off! *The sensitive or low self-esteem dog is not a shy dog; he simply needs to know that he has your approval.*

Basis for the Behavior of the Dog with Low Self-Esteem

This is a dog that thinks a great deal of you and constantly worries about having your approval. This is not the result of training, but a part of the natural makeup of these types of dogs. The constant need for approval usually indicates a level of confidence that is very low. This type of dog needs a lot of encouragement and an upbeat atmosphere to know that he is doing things right.

This dog also frequently has a low pain threshold. For instance, if he gets hit by a sheep, it appears to hurt him more than it does the less-sensitive dog. This dog has already undervalued himself and has a low confidence level, and on top of that, he got hit! It can deflate whatever confidence he had in the first place and turn him off. Be careful not to place this kind of dog in situations where this could happen in the early stages of training.

Working with the Dog with Low Self-Esteem

Most dogs of this type can be turned into useful, confident workers. They do not have to remain wallflowers for life! You have to stay upbeat, but gradually teach the sensitive, low self-esteem dog to take correction. In order to achieve his potential, any dog must be able to take correction. This dog must learn that being corrected doesn't mean you disapprove of him. You still like or love this dog and want him to work, but you have the right, as owner and handler, to tell him what to do. This will not happen quickly and is a long-term investment in training.

If you are shopping for a pup and one of the parents appears to be a dog of this personality type, I would advise you to find another litter from which to choose. But if you already own a dog with low self-esteem, and this is the dog you love and want to work, you should know that he can be made into a useful and enjoyable partner.

Many of these personality traits may disappear as you train and instill confidence in your dog. This dog's ability may surface as you build trust in him and his trust in you. With the proper work and use of this training program, you can turn your dog into a confident worker that won't be run off the field by any sheep. Once self-confidence rises, this dog can be downright pushy!

Often, once this type of dog becomes confident and is able to go right in and grip, he will tend to hang on a little bit longer than necessary. After taking hold, he may not know exactly what to do. It's like the old adage about dogs that chase cars—if they ever catch one, they may not know what to do with it!

So once your dog will get in and grip, it is time to get into close quarters and do some close-contact work (see chapter 6). Be sure that you don't do this too early when your dog does not have the confidence to handle it. Practice it only after your dog develops some confidence.

Another thing you often will see in the dog of this personality type is a possible fearfulness to walk in on the sheep at first. Be sure to work very quiet, dog-broke sheep at first and give a lot of encouragement and coaxing for the dog to come in close. Quiet, dog-broke sheep will keep the dog from being beaten up and run over and will help you keep an orderly situation. These dogs like order and become extremely uncomfortable if things get out of hand and out of their control.

It is important to build self-esteem with everything you do with this dog. For instance, even when petting, encourage him to stand up rather than lie down to be petted. Encourage looking you in the eye instead of turning his head away or looking down. Never pet this type of dog on the top of the head. Pet or rub him on the chest or underneath the chin and neck to help draw him up to a standing position.

THE LAID-BACK DOG

Characteristics of the Laid-Back Dog

The laid-back dog is one that is not enthusiastic in his approach to work. It is important to determine if your dog is not enthusiastic because of not having a strong desire to work, or if this dog was improperly handled or intimidated to the point that he does not *want* to work stock. Dogs that have been improperly handled or intimidated may want to avoid making eye contact with the stock.

Some breeds other than the Border Collie may be particularly prone to exhibit this lack of enthusiasm and intensity because they may not have been bred for instinct and natural ability. However, if there is some degree of instinct present, many of these dogs can be brought along to the point that they will stay out in the field and work for a handler they love and respect.

The laid-back dog may be extremely hard to work because of being easily distracted and not readily concentrating on the stock. You may repeatedly have to call this dog back to the stock if he is distracted by smells, other dogs or anything of more interest than the stock.

This type of dog is not likely to make a top trial dog because of a lack of enthusiasm and intensity. The degree of obedience and authority you may have to exert to get him to perform at a high level may discourage this dog from working. This, coupled with an already low level of enthusiasm, may result in "turning off" (not wanting to work at all). But he may make a good farm dog because of not being likely to "worry" the stock all the time. He may be glad to work when you ask, but equally glad to stop working. If you are careful not to get your dog in situations over his head or beyond his ability, he may become a very useful farm dog.

Basis for the Behavior of the Laid-Back Dog

The basis for the distractability, lack of interest, lack of enthusiasm and lack of intensity in the laid-back dog is often a low level of instinct for working stock. This is usually the result of a poor breeding program with regard to selection for herding ability. If you want a working dog, look for good working parents and a reputable breeder!

If the dog's behavior is the result of poor handling or being intimidated by overly aggressive stock during early training, the laid-back dog's attitude may or may not be possible to overcome.

Working with the Laid-Back Dog

Unless the dog completely ignores the stock, it is likely that he can be trained to make use of and maximize whatever degree of instinct and ability he possesses. It will take a lot of time and patience. You will have to read your dog carefully so he does not turn off. But as he gains confidence in himself and in you, he will likely come along.

It is important to keep variety in his training program to keep him interested. If your dog is only 20 percent enthusiastic, compared to what you would like him to be, you will have to make up for the 80 percent enthusiasm that he is lacking!

The laid-back dog should follow the general training program. Be aware that you will not be able to drill repeatedly on exercises or tasks because this dog lacks enthusiasm. Therefore, it may be that some exercises will require a long time for the dog to learn, simply because you cannot repeat them frequently during a single session.

Giving the dog work that is perceived as useful and fun will help improve his attitude. "Read" your dog and see what he appears to enjoy. Use the work the dog appears to enjoy the most in between those things that are less enjoyable.

If your dog is also very sensitive to authority or has low self-esteem, remember to praise frequently and enthusiastically when he is performing well so that your dog will know that you approve of his behavior.

A laid-back dog and a handler that understands this dog's personality, as well as the need for enthusiasm and praise often, are able to perform a variety of tasks and enjoy herding for farm work or as a hobby.

THE EXCESSIVELY PRESSURE-SENSITIVE DOG

Characteristics of the Excessively Pressure-Sensitive Dog

This type of dog is overly sensitive to pressures exerted by the sheep and/or the handler. That is, this dog *overreacts* to pressure. The degree of being excessively sensitive or overreacting may vary.

The excessively pressure-sensitive dog is usually very anxious about keeping the sheep together and interprets *any* movement, however slight, as necessitating a response. He does not understand *how* to respond and may continually move around the sheep and refuse to take directions from the handler. The dog may grip frequently, especially going in his uncomfortable direction. He is typically difficult to stop or, if stopped, will seldom stay stopped for more than a few seconds.

This type of dog may be the dog that you will find chained up at a farm for his entire life because the handler/owner claims the dog is "unmanageable." He is not really unmanageable—the handler just didn't understand the basis for this type of dog's behavior and wasn't knowledgeable about how to work with it.

Basis for the Behavior of the Excessively Pressure-Sensitive Dog

This dog's behavior is based on the principle that every action has an overreaction. That is, for most dogs, action by the sheep should generate an equal and opposite reaction, but this particular type of dog tends to overreact in most situations.

Practically all dogs, when you first start them, will have an element of excessive sensitivity to pressure. Even though you think the dog is working on you, he will be working on the heads of the sheep. If you don't believe it, leave the field and see if your dog pushes the sheep as close as he can get them to you. Probably not. Instead, he will stop the sheep on any part of the fence they happen to come to! This shows that, at first, you are not a part of the game plan. It is extremely important that you *become* a part of the game plan and *make* yourself a part of that plan so that, as soon as possible, the dog *will* work on you.

This dog overreacts to pressure and can't help himself. He is so attuned to pressure during early training that he can't stop himself from reacting and feels as though he would *die* without reacting to it! So the slightest movement or change in body language of the sheep causes a reaction from the dog. Even if the dog is lying down, if the sheep move in any way—a flick of the ear, a shift of weight, a turn of the head—the dog must react.

This type of dog also may overreact to the handler's body language. You may have to stand like a statue to keep the dog in one place. If you shift from one foot to another the dog will react and be on his way to try to re-establish balance. Once the dog reaches the balance point, he often is too close and will push the sheep one way or the other, instantly creating an imbalance, necessitating a reaction to it.

This may be one of the hardest types of dogs with which you will ever work, because this dog feels like his reactions are part of a life-or-death situation. It is important to realize that this type of dog is not really pushy and is not trying to take advantage of you. He simply feels *compelled* to respond to the slightest pressures generated by the sheep and/or handler.

Working with the Excessively Pressure-Sensitive Dog

If you try to come down too hard you may do one of two things: (1) force the dog to fight or try to beat you, or (2) shut him right down (make him not want to work the stock). Instead of being too forceful with this dog, remember that you have the chance to create a very valuable and useful partner for working on your farm or a potential winner in trial competition. It requires a bit of work to quiet this dog down and get him to be a good trial dog, but it is definitely possible.

I have found that many dogs of this personality type are very one-sided. They are excessively sensitive anyway, but you might say they are super-excessively sensitive or *terribly uncomfortable* going in one direction.

In training this type of dog it helps to have your dog know the command "Lie Down" before he begins working with stock. It is important that you be able to identify the side on which he is most uncomfortable, usually that side where he works closest to the sheep and where he grips most often. It also is important that you have thoroughly dog-broke sheep that will stay close to you.

Your primary goals in working with this dog will be to help him become comfortable and less anxious about the movements of the sheep, to have him learn to work on you instead of the sheep and to teach him to stay off the sheep.

Training Exercises for the Excessively Pressure-Sensitive Dog

Continuous Movement While Turning

This exercise is aimed at getting the dog to be relaxed and comfortable around the sheep, to work on you (instead of just the sheep) and to "balance up the sides" by having the dog move in his nonpreferred (uncomfortable) direction.

For purposes of example, consider a dog that is most uncomfortable going in a clockwise ("Come Bye") direction. You will wear in a clockwise circle that is 6 to 8 yards in diameter, letting the sheep follow you and letting the dog try to re-establish balance (stop the movement of the sheep). Your job is to make sure he never makes it!

If the dog starts to run faster, make the circle smaller and keep turning; if the dog starts to widen out where he belongs, then you can make your circle bigger.

You do *not* want to change the direction of the circle. Keep following the circle on the uncomfortable side of the dog. Keep your eye on the dog. If he starts to come by you ("lap" you on the circle), turn a little more sharply, take your crook or boogie bag and slap the ground lightly to make him fade back. The dog's own centrifugal force, created by the attempt to re-establish balance while circling, will help push him out.

I have found that it is a waste of time to try to push these dogs out yourself by use of aggressive body language and the crook. The dog becomes *so* uncomfortable with the environment created to push him out that he will beat you at your own game. He will fly through you, go around you or do anything to get to the sheep! So the best thing you can do is to start walking in tight or wider circles as described above.

On a cold day, when your dog is not going to overheat, you may have to walk continuously for thirty to forty-five minutes. If it is a warm day, of course, you must limit the time because of the possibility of heat exhaustion. Remember, your dog is running all the time you are walking!

Every time the dog starts to come past you, just cut your turn toward the sheep more sharply. Every time the dog widens out, make your circle a little larger. Keep walking! Do not stop. Do not change directions. Do not have the dog lie down. By turning in a circle the dog gradually finds himself working and balancing on you instead of the sheep. This may, at first, seem foreign to you. I'd be surprised if anyone has ever told you to do this before. But take my word for it, it *will* work.

You must not do it halfway! You must walk until the dog has either reached the point of exhaustion or has reached the point that he is tired enough to fall back and widen out. Then you will find that you will be able to stop and tell the dog to lie down. If you have done your work properly and the dog is tired enough, he will lie down and stay there. He will be at a balance point and will be tired and comfortable enough to lie down and stay down. This may be the first time since you have started working that you have actually seen this dog relaxed and comfortable around the sheep! This is your first major step toward training this type of dog. End the lesson here; call the dog off and leave the field. You are now on the road to winning with this dog and having an enjoyable and useful partner.

Continuing Work with the Excessively Pressure-Sensitive Dog

It is important that you work this type of dog again the next day. Go back out, have the dog lie down, go to the sheep and start wearing again in your dog's uncomfortable direction. As before, avoid wearing in a straight line.

By continually turning, you keep the balance uneven. The dog will constantly try to re-establish or reach the balance point, having something to do and think about. Because the dog is constantly working, he is not as likely to come in and grip. The dog will also feel good about himself!

By the third lesson, you will start by continuing to turn and walk in the dog's uncomfortable direction. After five minutes or so, you can test whether you may be ready to go to the next step by turning to your dog and telling him to lie down. If your dog lies down quietly and contentedly, and is willing to stay down, he is becoming comfortable with this environment. The dog is also beginning to realize that he should be working on you. You will notice this when he cares about where you are.

If your dog dropped willingly and is comfortable, it is time to start circling in the other direction. Turn circles in this direction for several minutes and then tell the dog to lie down. If he is not comfortable and does not lie down, or lies down and then jumps right back up again to work another pressure point, start turning again until the dog gets comfortable with it. Spend another five to ten minutes before telling him to lie down again.

Remember that your "Lie Down" command should be quiet and that you should not have to yell. You want the dog to understand working quietly and that you can communicate with *quiet commands*.

Once the dog lies down readily and is comfortable in this direction, start again in the uncomfortable direction. If he starts to come in a little too close while you are turning, say "Get Out" while continuing to turn. This will force him out farther and farther. If you keep turning according to the procedure described above, very few dogs will continue to come in tighter and tighter. Most will gradually widen out. The dog will begin to be comfortable farther out from the sheep. The continual turning will help the dog to work and balance on you.

Progression of Work

As you continue to work your dog using this method, you will begin dropping your dog more often. It is critical that you stop your dog *only on balance*. After the drop, reverse the direction in which you are turning and start again. Gradually decrease your number of turns before dropping. Be careful to help the dog stay out from the sheep, but do not get after him severely to get out like you would with other dogs. For dogs that are *not* excessively pressure-sensitive, you might use slapping the crook or the boogie bag on the ground to force them out. However, that action only gets *this* type of dog more riled up and encourages them to try to beat you at your own game'' and get at the sheep because they feel they have to.

Remember that this dog is not intentionally trying to cheat or misbehave. He is trying very hard to do everything you want, but he does not know *how* to do it. It is just that this dog is *so* sensitive to pressure that it is almost an affliction! He feels he must react or die!

By continually turning, as described here, the excessively pressure-sensitive dog will come to feel comfortable at a balance point and comfortable balancing upon you. Eventually he will be able to wear in serpentines, maintaining a comfortable distance from the sheep and a constant radius on the turns. If after a couple of loops on a serpentine, you see that your dog is beginning to get tense or jittery, start turning in your clockwise circles again for several minutes until he quiets down again. Then drop the dog and start again with the serpentines. This should all be slow work without any fast moves or "hurry up" around the flanks.

Adding Outruns, Stops and Flanking Work

With consistent work, the dog will eventually begin to be relaxed most of the time and comfortable going either clockwise or counterclockwise. Whenever he gets tense in any way, go into the continually turning circle routine. Once the dog is relaxed and comfortable going in both directions, then you can begin adding other training exercises, such as outruns, stops and wearing. You can begin flanking work by stepping over and encouraging your dog to come around you using the Handler-to-Side Outrun (refer back to Diagram 16). The "shot-gun" or Sling-Shot Outruns (refer back to Diagram 19) are particularly good for this dog because they give him a lot of action and allow venting of some intense desire. Delay setting the dog up next to you for an outrun for quite a long time.

Progress with Wearing

Most excessively pressure-sensitive dogs at this point *still* will not like to wear in a straight line for very long. They can't stand this kind of "prosperity"! They do not know how to react when they reach the balance and the sheep begin coming straight to you.

If you find that your dog gets nervous after doing a little wearing in a straight line, quickly drop him. Call him off and do a little outrun or some turning or serpentines to get your dog settled back down again. As time goes on (weeks to months), the wears should be getting longer, quieter and easier.

Driving

Once the dog has settled down fairly well, and is doing the exercises quietly and with some confidence, you will be ready to start doing some driving. Don't allow too much time to go by before starting to drive. If you let wearing and gathering become too much of an imprinted habit, it will be more difficult to get this type of dog to drive. Because of being excessively sensitive, any habit becomes a "super-habit," that is more deeply ingrained, more quickly than with a dog that is not excessively sensitive.

As described in chapter 5, start driving with your dog on a long line. Remember to start with very short distances—perhaps only 3 feet or 4 feet at first. As with all dogs, be sure to break up the drive and the fetch to avoid the formation of bad habits.

Helping the Excessively Pressure-Sensitive Dog Learn to Be Comfortable When Working Close

At this point, let us assume that your dog is able to do outruns well, kick out and stay off the sheep and work well while staying off the sheep. These have been major undertakings for this dog! Let us also assume that this dog is so well balanced that he can do outruns in both directions and drive and flank on each side. He may still want to grip if the sheep do not move off quickly at the top of the outrun because of coming in close at that time. At this point, you have a dog that is only comfortable when working *away* from the sheep. It is now time to do some close-contact work (see chapter 6).

You have to *teach* this same dog to be comfortable in an uncomfortable environment—to be able to work in close! He has to learn this to pull sheep off of fences and out of corners, to work in close areas, to take sheep or other stock off of trucks or trailers; in other words, to get into areas where he just doesn't like to be. For the excessively pressure-sensitive dog, this is *extremely* difficult! The dog has to learn to control emotions and to have confidence in his ability to move sheep slowly and deliberately without flying in and gripping. Mastering close-contact work will provide you both with increased confidence in your abilities to handle any situation.

THE INTENSE DOG

Characteristics of the Intense Dog

The intense or keen dog falls somewhere between the laid-back dog at one extreme and the hard dog at the other. The intense dog is closer to the hard dog than to the laid-back dog, but is not as dominant an individual as the hard dog.

This dog is characterized by an intense desire to work stock and is not able to relax when around stock, a factor that may be detrimental if present in the extreme. He *can* relax when away from the stock.

He may or may not have a lot of natural ability to accompany a

Intense dogs are easy to train in some respects, since they are always ready to work and tend to have a natural ability to balance. They are usually quick to understand what is wanted.

desire to work. But if natural ability is present with a moderate degree of keenness, the intense dog is often very athletic and eager to learn.

This dog is "pushy" because of wanting to get things done in a hurry, and will be less careful than the talented dog. He will tend to work close to the stock until taught to keep a distance.

This dog does not know what it means to be too tired or too sick to work! He is always "on" and ready to work. He is often very athletic and will work into old age with a good attitude. The intense dog is often a good dog for such work as loading stock into chutes, pens or trailers, since he does not give ground naturally—he will walk in and hold his ground.

Basis for the Behavior of the Intense Dog

The basis for the dog's behavior lies in his *extreme* desire to work stock and tendency to want to get things done in a hurry! Because of this intensity, this dog will tend to be pushy.

Working with the Intense Dog

The intense dog is easy to train in some respects since he is always ready to work and tends to have a natural ability to balance. He usually is quick to understand what is wanted.

However, at the same time, a dog of this personality may be a challenge because of wanting to "walk on you" or do things his own way all the time. He tends to second-guess you and anticipate continually. Because you did one thing a certain way yesterday, he will think that you will want to the same thing the same way today. If you are headed for a gate, this dog will want to be there ahead of you and be the first one through it. He can create some problems for both of you because of this!

Because the dog wants to get things done in a hurry, you will continually need to slow him down and help him learn to take time and be deliberate while working. The initial training is especially important in establishing the habit of working slowly and deliberately, although you may have to deal with his tendency to want to do things rapidly throughout his life.

In addition, because he tends to work close to the stock, you will need to be conscientious about widening him out and getting him to recognize and maintain a proper "comfort zone." If natural ability is present, most intense dogs will easily learn to have good square flanks and have good or great outruns in a desirable pear-shaped pattern.

Because of a tendency for this dog to be pushy, you may have to come down very hard to get him to listen. This may be problematic because he may become very intimidated temporarily because of the severity of the correction. So read your dog and lighten up after a severe correction if he becomes excessively intimidated.

Training Exercises for the Intense Dog

The intense or keen dog will need to master all of the areas and exercises described for the training program.

Areas of special importance with the intense dog include the exercises for widening out (see chapter 5) and encouraging slow work by learning "Steady" (see chapter 4).

CONCLUSION

Your dog will show tendencies toward one or more of the personality types and traits described in this chapter. Knowing about the personality types that your dog displays will enable you to better understand him and the bases for his behavior, and to approach his training efficiently and effectively. You will not only maximize the dog's potential, but will more likely be able to produce positive experiences that will make herding an enjoyable activity for both you and your dog!

The combination of herding personality types and traits in each dog is the source of individual variation that makes each dog unique. Learning about your dog and yourself and how your personalities can complement each other as a team is an exciting challenge for continuous improvement throughout the life of your dog.

8

Working Different Kinds of Stock

"The material of thinking is not thoughts, but actions, facts, events and the relations of things."

John Dewey, *Learning as Problem Solving*

OVERVIEW

Herding dogs may be used to work many types of livestock. This book deals primarily with working sheep since this is the type of stock I recommend using for training herding dogs. This chapter will discuss working cattle and poultry, desirable characteristics in dogs that are intended to work these types of stock and special considerations about training your dog to work with these animals.

The American Kennel Club (AKC), Australian Shepherd Club of America (ASCA) and American Herding Breeds Association (AHBA) offer options for tests or trials on cattle, ducks and sheep.

GENERAL STOCK KNOWLEDGE

Regardless of the type of stock you work, you need to become knowledgeable about other stock, the ways in which they typically react and how to read them. This is a vital part of training and handling your dog when working a particular type of animal. Knowledge of the stock and its behavior in different situations also contributes to maintaining the safety of the stock, your dog and yourself.

With large or potentially wild animals, such as cattle, safety for you and your dog are major considerations. With poultry, safety for the dog and the stock are the main concerns.

WORKING CATTLE

Behavior of Cattle

Cattle have more of a tendency to spread out than sheep. Once they are used to being worked, cattle will move as easily as, or more easily than, sheep. But some cattle may fight the dog more than sheep will, and they may not give up as easily.

Be aware that your dog will likely take some bumps from cattle. Avoid letting your dog get caught in corners where he cannot escape. If caught in a corner by a wise old cow, your dog may get hurt or even killed.

Behavior of the Dog When Working Cattle

The dog must work harder to put cattle together and must be more aggressive than when working sheep. She must have a lot of heart because cattle are naturally more aggressive. The dog will have to work closer to the cattle to move them and will have to be more harsh and take some nips at them. It takes a dog with a special ability to work cattle. Not all dogs are cut out for it.

It is desirable to have a "low-bite dog" for working cattle. Having a "low bite" means that your dog will bite low down by the dewclaws or heels of the cattle. If she bites high (up by the hocks of the cows) the dog will raise her head and expose neck and chest, leaving her vulnerable to kicks and blows from the cows. If she bites low, the cow will kick over the top of the dog without making contact. Some good cattle dogs will splay their front legs to the ground and duck as they bite in order to avoid being kicked.

Starting Your Dog on Cattle

I believe your dog should have some experience working sheep before being introduced to cattle. This way she will already have an idea about what the job is and be able to work with you to get it done. But if you do not have access to sheep and must start your dog on cattle from the first, it can be done.

Always start your dog on cattle that are not aggressive. Heifers or young steers usually are good. Try to avoid using older cows or bulls. If the cattle you are working have never been worked with dogs, you will have to be more careful than if the cattle are accustomed to stock dogs.

As a general rule, the young dog of gathering breeds will have much more power when bringing the cows *to* you (gathering them) than when driving them away from you. Older dogs that already know how to drive or the breeds that prefer to drive will have a lot of power when pushing stock away from you. Remember this when you are starting your dog, and let natural style help her move the cows.

Because cattle are larger and taller and because the dog is working close to them, you will not be able to see the dog as easily as you do

Some cattle may fight the dog more than sheep will, and cattle may not give up as easily.

185

The dog will have to work closer to the cattle to move them and will have to be more harsh and take some nips at them.

when working sheep. Therefore, you will have to watch and read their heads and their reactions to know where the dog is and what she is most likely doing.

It may be extremely hard to teach your dog to wear properly when working cattle. It is not a problem to have the beginning dog hold the sheep to you and to have the sheep stay close. With cattle, this is a

It takes a dog with a special ability to work cattle—not all dogs are cut out for it.

problem, since cattle do not naturally follow like sheep do. Later in training, when the dog has learned to hold a comfort zone and give the stock some breathing room so that they do not have to be on top of the handler, this is less of a problem. At that stage, cattle can be given enough distance and wearing is possible and practical.

WORKING POULTRY

Dogs may be used to work a variety of types of poultry, including ducks, chickens and turkeys. I will focus primarily on the working of ducks, but will comment on other types of poultry as well.

Behavior of Ducks

Ducks tend to flock or stay in a group when being worked. Sometimes a wise old duck that is used to being worked will learn to split off and take off every chance she gets. Another trick that ducks may learn is to stick their heads through woven wire fencing in order to resist being moved. Some breeds of ducks, like the Muscovy, may

Dogs may be used to work a variety of types of poultry, including ducks, chickens and turkeys.

"play dead" and then fly up into the face of the dog, a tactic that may be very startling to a young dog.

Ducks do not tend to become as handler-oriented as sheep and, although they will group, do not tend to come to and stay with the handler like sheep. Also, they are more difficult to hold still in an area for practicing outruns or fence-line pickups. One thing you can try in order to hold ducks in a specific place is to put out a small amount of feed. This can help keep them interested in staying in one place while you set up an exercise.

Behavior of the Dog When Working Ducks

Dogs usually must work much closer on ducks than on sheep. One reason I do not advocate starting young dogs on ducks is that they may get in a bad habit of working very close to the stock. But if you have a dog that is initially intimidated by sheep or that does not show a lot of interest in sheep, it may be preferable to start on ducks. The different type of movement and small size of ducks may help "turn on" the instinct in some dogs that may not have shown interest in sheep.

If you do start your dog on ducks, try to start working on sheep as quickly as possible unless you plan to work *only* poultry.

Behavior of Turkeys

Turkeys are known to panic at the drop of a hat! They may run into a corner and pile up, and, in extreme cases, suffocate. A quiet, well-trained dog may be able to work turkeys and cause even less panic than a human being.

Behavior of Chickens

Chickens can be a lot of fun to work. They move easily and are fast, but may not flock as well as ducks.

9

Special Problems

"We must know what things cause before we know what causes things."

J. M. Innes, veterinary pathologist

OVERVIEW

This chapter will deal with special problems that may or may not arise during your herding training. These problems may be specific to certain breeds, or may deal with habits or tendencies of dogs to work in certain ways. In addition, some areas related to general dog behavior and living with your herding dog will be covered.

DOG WORKS TOO WIDE OR TOO FAR OFF THE SHEEP

This problem is sometimes seen in Border Collies but seldom, if ever, in other herding breeds. If you know the bloodlines of your dog and/or that one or both parents is a wide-swinging dog, you may realize that you have the potential for this problem when starting your young dog. If this is the case, be careful about widening this young dog out very much or too quickly. If you begin to intimidate the dog, he may get wider than you want.

189

Here the author demonstrates the concepts of pressure and balance, using a magnetic board to represent the positions of dog and sheep.

Many dogs that widen out naturally have a lot of eye. They naturally do square flanks. When faced with a problem, their tendency is to swing out and regroup. They tend to want to do their own thinking, and may not always want to follow your directions. For intermediate and advanced training, a "Come In" command or whistle may be useful.

This type of dog is usually very attuned to pressure and works very deliberately. It is up to you to take some of this deliberate nature out, and have the dog move when you ask. He may tend to "lock up" instead of reacting when you ask him to move. It is important that the dog learn "Walk In" when you tell him, rather than becoming mesmerized because of a strong eye. If you do not allow the wideness, strong eye and deliberateness to become excessive and to become bad habits, you will have an excellent dog that is a joy to work!

When your outruns get to be 200 to 300 yards in length, sometimes this type of dog may kick *too far* out. This problem may be compounded by your having widened out this type of dog too much during early training. Sending this type of dog on the outrun with a "*Sh-h-h-h,*" rather than a directional command, may help send him along a straighter path and decrease some of the wideness. A "Come In" whistle may be used to help bring the dog in once he has started on the outrun. *However, using such a whistle will result in a point deduction in a herding trial.*

Sometimes this type of dog will shut down early during an outrun when close to a fence and feeling pressure from the sheep. In this situation the dog is uncomfortable about trying to get past the sheep and feels a need to be farther out. You must force him to pass that pressure point or wall of pressure that he is feeling and get him around behind the sheep. In other words, you must help this dog learn to be more comfortable while working close to the sheep.

DOG IS EXTREMELY HEAVY ON ONE SIDE

A really heavy, one-sided dog may be a real problem! If you have trouble getting your dog to go around on his bad side, don't allow this dog to work only in his preferred direction. This just reinforces the preferred direction and will make it more and more difficult to get the dog going the other way. If you can't make him go in the nonpreferred direction, get some help! The sooner you can get this problem remedied, the better.

Don't let yourself get mad and end up yelling and screaming at your dog. This will just cause extra anxiety and confusion and may start a bad habit of gripping. See chapter 3 for ways to get the very one-sided dog to go in the nonpreferred direction. You will constantly have to be aware of your dog's strengths and weaknesses, and always practice more on the weak side.

DOG WORKS TOO TIGHT

This can be a problem with Border Collies, but is more prominent in other breeds of herding dogs. It is important to get your dog off of the stock and widened out. But be careful to read your dog. If not very keen to work, the dog may end up giving up on working stock. **READ YOUR DOG!** Gently but firmly push him out, call him back to work, if needed, and help your dog learn "stick-to-it-iveness" while working.

Border Collies usually are intense enough to be widened out within several lessons. Because of their high level of intensity, most Belgians and some Australian Shepherds must be widened out very early in training. Other breeds may need to be widened out more gradually. Finding the correct degree of "intimidation" is the key!

DOG IS HARD TO STOP

During early stages of training, difficulty in stopping your dog may be the result of improper handling or positioning. During the early stages of training, be sure that you are at the balance point when asking your dog to lie down. You may need to use the long line to enforce your "Lie Down" command. Make sure you time your command so that the dog hears it just before hitting the end of the line! During early training, do not insist that the dog stay down once stopped—have him get right back up and get back to work. Then as your training proceeds, you can gradually increase the length of time during which the dog stays stopped and lying down. If you insist on staying down too long very early in training, you may find that your dog will become *harder* to stop, not easier! It may just agitate the dog and make him more inclined to disobey.

If your dog is well along in training and will not stop, it may be that you will need to back up and do some work at short distances from the sheep, requiring your dog to stop off balance. Review the Daisy Wheel Pattern (refer back to Diagram 18) and use this exercise to help establish your authority.

If your dog is hard to stop at the top of a longer outrun, it may be of benefit for you to run to and through the sheep with "calculated anger," surprising your dog with your presence and a firm "Lie Down."

Some breeds of dogs may be particularly hard to stop. For instance, German Shepherd Dogs may find lying down to be very degrading. They are not natural "clappers" (dogs that lie down quickly and easily). Because of their size, many German Shepherd Dogs and other large breeds get tired of getting up and down repeatedly. Bouviers des Flandres also may resist lying down. Many Shetland Sheepdogs do not like to lie down and may prefer to sit. I do not like the way this looks and prefer that they *also* learn to stop on their feet. For all of these types of dogs, a "Stand, Stay" command is preferred. Teaching this command may require some time and initially should be taught while away from the stock.

OUTRUNS ARE TOO TIGHT

To address this problem, you must have enough control to stop while your dog is on the way out. You need to be able to stop whenever the dog begins to be incorrect. For example, if you are sending your dog on an outrun in the "Away to Me" direction and he starts to cut in, you will need to stop him. Then position yourself extremely off balance to your dog, toward the sheep and to your left. Give the command "Get Out, Away to Me." This correction builds on the "Get Out" exercise and work that should have been done earlier in training. You may have to back up and teach or remind the dog what the "Get Out" reprimand means if he does not readily obey when you try a correction on the outrun.

DOG WILL NOT COME WHEN CALLED

If your dog will not come to you either on or away from the sheep, the problem probably stems from puppyhood. At approximately sixteen weeks of age, most puppies will challenge your authority and begin to ignore or disobey you when you tell them "That'll Do, Here" to get them to come. This is the time to make sure that you use a long line and let your dog know that you have a much longer arm than he thought! If you do not do this, if you continually allow him to "cheat" and not come to you when asked to do so at an early age, then you are setting yourself up to have a lifelong problem.

If your dog will come to you when away from the stock, but does not come off the stock when called, this may result from a strong desire to work and to obey instinct over command. Follow the instructions for calling your dog off, as outlined in chapter 3. Be sure you have the long line on the dog so that you can enforce this.

Remember to include call-offs frequently during your work and not just at the end of the training session. Pull your dog off of the sheep and then send him to gather the sheep again. This helps promote a good attitude when coming off the sheep because sometimes the dog will get to work the sheep again, and that pulling off does not always mean an end to the fun.

DOG WILL NOT MAINTAIN THE "COMFORT ZONE"

Maintaining a comfort zone is not natural for many dogs and must be *taught*. It is taught by what we call "intimidation." Take the boogie bag or crook and *make* your dog *believe* that he might actually be struck! Therefore the dog must be wary. As you are wearing, slap the crook or boogie bag on the ground, telling the dog "Get Out of that!" Use a deep, forceful voice to show that you mean business. Follow through and enforce the intimidation by backing the dog off or you running through the sheep at him, if necessary. If the sheep are at your feet or trying to push past you, your dog must learn that he can't just keep pushing them and must back off. See chapter 5 for a review of these techniques.

DOG GRIPS (BITES) WHILE WORKING STOCK

"Grip" is the term used by stockdog handlers to mean "bite." In farm situations or in moving cattle this may be necessary, but *in sheep herding trials, grips are not allowed*. The only exception is in situations when the dog needs to fend off an angry, charging old ewe or ram. So gripping must be "taken out of the dog" as quickly as possible, but in such a way as to *leave the ability to grip, but remove the desire to do so*. The dog must know that, if things get too tough, he has the *alternative* to grip. If not left with this knowledge, most likely your dog will not have the confidence or power to move sheep properly. It is extremely important *how* you take the grip out of the dog; you must do it properly, and relatively quickly, but not so quickly that you lose something in the process.

Reasons for Gripping

There are many different types of grips and many different reasons why a dog grips. Grips may occur because a dog is strong-eyed ("sticky"), one-sided, bored, generally uncomfortable or excessively sensitive to pressure. They may occur in a young dog because of lack of training or in an older dog because they have become a habit.

It is important to understand why the grips are occurring, what happens when the grip occurs and if it is your fault. I find that, in a lot of cases, the grips occur because you have positioned *yourself*

194

improperly, putting the dog at a disadvantage, and thus inviting a grip. There may be certain areas or situations in which the dog is very uncomfortable with the environment, and therefore more likely to grip. Teaching a dog to be comfortable in his environment is extremely important. You have to set the stage to avoid a grip when the dog is uncomfortable and therefore eliminate the discomfort so that the dog will not have to bite. Then as you keep working at it, you can make the situations gradually more difficult, so that the dog learns to cope with these situations, builds confidence and stops gripping.

You must *teach* that you do not want the grip, as it will not disappear on its own. It may start as a reflection of discomfort, but may quickly become a habit. Once it becomes a habit, it will be harder to eliminate.

Gripping and the Strong-Eyed Dog

If you work with stock dogs for any length of time, you will run into strong-eyed or "sticky" dogs. The Border Collie is one of the few breeds that shows a lot of "eye" and the majority of sticky dogs therefore will be Border Collies.

These dogs become almost mesmerized by the sheep. This trance-like behavior seems to be from having the dog's *total* attention on the sheep. Usually the dog will be looking at the sheep with a moderate amount of "eye," but when you speak, you *will* be able to get the dog's attention. With the strong-eyed dog, when you speak you will *not* be able to get his attention. This dog will be so locked into eyeing the sheep, so mesmerized by watching and looking into the eyes of the sheep or at their movement, that he won't even be conscious that you are present!

It is extremely important that you get a part of the strong-eyed dog's brain to *want* to listen to what you have to say. This is a giant step in correcting the strong-eyed dog. When you do break the strong-eyed dog out of the trance, he will sometimes not know what to do. Not all strong-eyed dogs react the same way. Some strong-eyed dogs, once you have broken the trance will kick out away from the sheep (desirable), but then become mesmerized again when they get within a few feet of the sheep. Other strong-eyed dogs, once you have broken the mesmerization, will fly in and grip or hit the sheep. Some people may think this is the reaction of a vicious dog, because they tend to hit *hard*! This dog tends to hit with the same degree of intensity as the fixation that "locked him up" in the first place! The hit happens because this dog does not understand either what he is doing or what you want. Once you break the dog out of this trance and break his eye contact, he does not know the next step. So you have to push him out off the sheep far enough so that you can break the close contact.

Most strong-eyed dogs are strong-eyed only when they get in close. This relates to the concept of having a comfort zone. The mesmerizing occurs when a strong-eyed dog is uncomfortable, because he is in too close and is not maintaining the comfort zone. This is a way of showing his discomfort.

Breaking the Trance of the Strong-Eyed Dog

You have to get part of the dog's consciousness to stay on you. The dog has to be taught not to allow his *complete* attention to be focused on the sheep. He must have a part of his brain always thinking about what you want and what orders are being given.

Teaching the dog to concentrate half on the sheep and half on the handler is the key to the "sticky" dog. I recommend that you use a boogie bag (see chapter 1). You will be able to project a lot of force, giving emphasis to your verbal commands, when you slap the bag on the ground.

Let's say you have asked the dog to go in a clockwise ("Come Bye") direction around the sheep and he has locked up or become "stuck" and does not respond to your command. You have probably asked the dog to move two or three times by this time and have not gotten a response. The amount of force that will be necessary to break this dog's sticky habit will depend on the sensitivity of the dog. It is important that you read the dog accurately and gauge his sensitivity. If you use too much force for a relatively sensitive dog, you may shut him down. So, as always, start with minimal force and work up from there *if* necessary.

Ease up to the dog's right side. The dog will be facing the sheep and you will be facing the dog, with your back to the sheep. You will have the boogie bag in your left hand so that it is near the right side of the dog. This positioning, with you facing *away* from the sheep and toward the dog, will help the dog understand the direction to go in order to balance. If you are facing toward the sheep, it is harder for the dog to understand which way to go. Next, you will say the dog's name and "Come Bye." He probably will not move and will remain locked onto the sheep.

If there is no response the second time you say the dog's name and "Come Bye," hit the boogie bag on the *ground* at the dog's right side as hard as you can! Make the bag really *slap* near the dog as you say "Come Bye." If the dog breaks out of this stare, he will likely fly around to the far side of the sheep *or* fly in and grip. If he flies in and grips, you have a major problem to contend with. It is not easy to address this problem because the dog usually flies in so quickly, but it is possible to get him back out again.

If the dog did *not* move when you slapped the boogie bag on the ground near him, then you have even *more* of a problem. This indicates a dog who is not terribly sensitive. The next step or action is a little harsher, but will not result in any damage to the dog. Set yourself up again, just as I have described. Stand a little closer to the dog, within a foot or so. Say his name and "Come Bye." If you say the dog's name and "Come Bye" a *second time* without any response, take the boogie bag and swipe it close to the side of his head. This *should* shock him out of the trance. If you do it properly and quickly, a *single swipe* of the boogie bag should be sufficient!

This action will have shocked the dog and made such an impression on him that he will always be wondering where you are and what you might want. At first, this may be an apprehensive type of wondering. The dog may be thinking, "Where is that handler? . . . The last time I let him get up close to me, did I ever get one right up beside my little ol' head!" However, this will eventually translate into a habit of always having you as a part of his consciousness. As harsh as this sounds, it is important that you do it and do it *early* so that stickiness (or any other bad tendency) does not become a habit. It is much harder to cure a habit than it is to cure an initial problem.

If your dog flies in and hits after being broken of his stickiness, remember that he is in too close and/or he does not know what the next step should be. It is up to you to teach this. To do this, you have to position yourself near the sheep. Every time you have your dog lie down, pull the sheep away from him so that there is an adequate comfort zone. Then send your dog around the sheep. If you want the dog to go in a clockwise or "Come Bye" direction, step to your left with the boogie bag in your left hand. Slap the bag on the ground and say "Come Bye." Be assured that he will react—he will remember the last time that bag slapped near or at his head!

It is highly probable that your dog will kick out just a bit to the "Come Bye" side and then fly into the sheep. It is up to *you* to get over to your right, between the dog and the sheep, *before* he can get into them! You might slap the bag on the ground or against his shoulder, whatever it takes to get him to get out and around to the other side of the sheep. Once he gets around to the other side of the sheep, try to have him lie down *immediately*. Then back the sheep away from the dog to re-establish a comfort zone, and do it again. Be ready to react quickly and cut across again. It is important that your dog does not beat you this time.

It is *extremely* important to have a very good "Lie Down"; you must be able to have your dog lie down *instantly* once on the other side of the sheep. This will prevent the dog from gaining momentum and running around and around trying to beat you to the sheep. *You must be quick!* If you feel that you are repeatedly losing, then try to get some help from a professional trainer. This habit will only get worse if you do not conquer it immediately.

Your reactions and timing must be precise. You must be able to blow the dog out *before* he hits; you must meet the dog and get him to the other side of the sheep and *instantly* make him lie down. *Handler timing is crucial to success when training stock dogs*, and it is especially so with this exercise. Do not become discouraged if you fail to be quick enough in your early attempts. It takes time and experience to develop these skills.

At this point, pull the sheep off a distance to break the contact with the dog, and do it again . . . and again and again, first one way (clockwise) and then the other (counterclockwise), aiming for about one-half of a circle at a time, continually blowing the dog out. You won't be able to blow him out all the way like you would with a "regular" (nonsticky) dog. By the second or third lesson you will have the regular dog pushed out to where he belongs and working smoothly within his comfort zone. However, within three to five lessons, the sticky dog usually will be swinging out off the sheep. You will be gratified to see how freely and easily the dog works once you back him off and he is within his comfort zone!

Your dog will have finally realized what you want and what instincts were trying to tell him. Herding instincts weren't telling him to go in and hit. The "kill mechanism" was triggered by his being too close, and overpowered the instinct to swing or flank around the sheep. Once he learns flanking is what *you* want and also what instinct was *really* telling him to do, your troubles with stickiness are basically over. Once he learns that *gripping* is *out*, *flanking* is *in* and that staying off the sheep is a necessity, he will begin to work fluidly and easily!

As long as you are careful over the next few months and give your dog plenty of space, he will not grip. Do not try to work off fences or in close-contact situations for a while. Picking sheep up off the fence asks a lot from this type of dog because he gets so uncomfortable in a tight situation. If you do have to bring sheep off of a fence, try to drop the dog just before the sheep are ready to bolt away from the fence, so that the sheep can ease off and give the dog sufficient space.

Gripping and the One-Sided Dog

Gripping also may be a problem in the dog that is one-sided, that is, very uncomfortable going one direction; see chapter 3 for an explanation of this tendency. A dog is more likely to move in close to the sheep, and therefore to grip, when circling in his uncomfortable direction.

Do not mistake gripping associated with going in an uncomfortable direction with a cheap shot grip. The underlying reason for this grip is that the dog is uncomfortable, just as with the strong-eyed grip. With the dog that is very uncomfortable going one direction, there is a touch of excessive sensitivity to balancing pressure. You will use the strategies described earlier (see chapter 3) for getting the one-sided dog to go in the uncomfortable direction: placing yourself extremely off balance, using a fence or pulling the sheep around the dog. In addition to dealing with this dog's one-sidedness, you will have to deal with the gripping.

The dog will probably want to go straight into the sheep or go around the outside edge of the group, grabbing a sheep's flank on the way. It is up to you to get between the dog and the sheep and slap the boogie bag or crook on the ground or beside his body or head, saying ''Get Out'' in a gruff, reprimanding voice. When your dog kicks away from the sheep just a bit, have him lie down. It is extremely important for you to *praise* the minute he lies down so that the dog understands he has done well. Praise quietly so that your dog does not get excited, but *be genuine in your appreciation* of the fact that he has gone around the sheep without gripping.

Then pull the sheep away and start your dog again. The first two or three times you will have him lie down quickly. The next few times, after being off the sheep a little, let him go maybe one, two or three turns around the sheep until the dog starts to get tight again. Then have him lie down. When he starts to move, it is important that you let him keep moving. If you do not, he will start to freeze up and lie down more than you want. So once the dog starts to move, keep pushing him out and away from the sheep. Swish the boogie bag or whatever it takes to get him off the sheep. Once off the sheep, show that you are pleased by saying "Good dog."

Extreme one-sidedness does not balance up in a week or two or even a month or two. It will take a long time and you will have to work diligently with the dog.

The most important thing to remember is: **Get the dog off the sheep**! The gripping will stop when the dog is off the sheep. You must get after the dog when he grips—holler "Get Out of that, you! What are you doing? Get Out of that!" Use the noise of the boogie bag or crook against the ground to get the dog's attention. This will teach that gripping is unacceptable.

I have had some dogs for whom it took a week of lessons just to get them to *go in the direction* they did not like—they were that one-sided! Usually when the dog *does* go in the uncomfortable direction, a grip is imminent because he is so close!

You should add more sheep once the dog is off the sheep and consistently go in the direction he does not like. I like to use up to sixty or eighty head of sheep with this type of dog. The large number of sheep requires the dog to make a bigger circle just to get around them. Because there is so much to occupy this dog's mind, he spends a lot *less* time trying to come in tight.

Be careful to keep your dog out from the sheep and under control. Don't let him keep increasing speed around the sheep; keep everything as slow and deliberate as you can.

The moment the dog starts to get out of control, have him lie down. Then reset the stage and start again. I have never had a one-sided dog that was not able to be "balanced up" on both sides. Of course, the more one-sided a dog is, the longer it will take. Because the dog will be doing outruns equally well in either direction, you may think you have him all balanced up. However, when you get ready to drive, the one-sidedness will surface again. You will have to work on balancing up your dog's sides again.

Try hard to understand your dog. I can't stress enough the importance of understanding what makes your dog tick! Once you understand your dog, you have a much better chance of stopping the gripping, or solving any other difficulty.

The Talented Dog That Grips Hard at "Face-Offs" with Sheep

Some talented dogs with a lot of balance, particularly those that tend to run wide, have a tendency to grip very hard when coming in close to sheep that are facing and challenging them. These dogs are more comfortable when working at a distance from the sheep. They do not have a problem with coming in close to the sheep as the sheep are moving away from them. But they tend to fly in and grip aggressively when they have to come in close to a sheep face-to-face.

This problem is best addressed during close-contact work. When a sheep wants to face and challenge, have the dog walk right up to the sheep's face. You may quietly ask the dog "Take her" or "Get her." If he starts to grip hard, restrain with the leash and caution, as described in the section on close-contact work (see chapter 6).

Dog Comes in and Grips for No Apparent Reason

This dog may have a bit of a short fuse, may be excessively sensitive to pressure, very one-sided or, for some reason, very uncomfortable. If this is occurring early in your dog's training, let him know you disapprove of gripping and follow the appropriate training techniques for the problems that are causing this. If your dog is at the intermediate or advanced stages of training, he may need close-contact work to address this problem. Sometimes you may have to intimidate this type of dog in some way in order to discourage gripping. You may have to squeeze his muzzle firmly in order to make an impression, while saying "No! Get Out of that!" Usually this will make the dog realize not to grip.

If your dog is gripping at the top of the outrun, it is likely that you have extended the length of your outrun too quickly. He is not maintaining the comfort zone while bringing the sheep to you. When the sheep start to run, he may blow in and grip from behind. So, you need to step back and fill in this hole in the basic training. Go back to short outruns during which you can control and teach him to bring the sheep in slowly, maintaining the comfort zone. As he masters the shorter distances, gradually increase the length of the outruns.

The dog may grip for no apparent reason if you have allowed the habit to develop. You may have failed to recognize when your placement or positioning created problems. It may be that you are placing your dog in a very uncomfortable position, or he may be bored with the type or duration of work that you are doing. Especially if early in your training, you may have been wearing in a straight line for too long without a turn. Turning will create an unequal pressure to be dealt with and this gives him something to do.

The one-sided dog may grip on his uncomfortable side. He needs to be forced to kick off the sheep going in the uncomfortable direction in order to create a more comfortable situation.

For all of these problems, widening the dog out (getting him off and away from the sheep) will be the most important factor in preventing gripping. This is accomplished through different degrees of intimidation. Be sure to read your dog and widen him out as soon as he is able to accept it.

DOG BARKS EXCESSIVELY WHILE WORKING STOCK

Barking may help a dog with limited power to move the sheep. During early training, barking may be a reflection of excitement or playing that decreases and/or disappears as the dog settles down to working. However, dogs that persist in barking after they are well along in training will usually continue to bark.

If you have enough control, you may be able to quiet your dog down with a command, such as ''Be Quiet'' or ''No Bark.'' Then he will quiet down because you have told him to do so, not because he doesn't want to bark. Nevertheless, your dog will be quiet.

Most Bearded Collies will be noisy dogs that seem to bark just to hear themselves or to argue with you! They may or may not quiet down with continued work. Most Shetland Sheepdogs and Australian Shepherds that start out barking will quiet down with continued work.

DOG WANTS TO COME PAST THE SHEEP WHILE WEARING

During early training in wearing, most dogs will be working more on the heads of the sheep than on you. They will be worried about the sheep escaping and want to come around to their heads in order to hold them together and immobile.

In order to prevent this and teach your dog to stay behind the sheep, switch your crook to whichever hand is toward the side your dog wants to come around. Slap it on the ground and say "Get Out of that" to get the dog back behind the sheep. With continued work, he will learn to stay back where he belongs and learn to work on you, rather than the heads of the sheep. It also will help to practice a lot of circles and serpentines while wearing.

Another reason the dog may try to come past the sheep while wearing may be that you have put too much command on too early, and your dog is more concerned with watching and coming to you than about working the sheep. This happens most often with dogs that are very sensitive to the handler, dogs that lack intensity and dogs that have hard personalities. They will be looking at you and walk right past the sheep! Do not use hand signals, swing your crook around or overcommand if this is the case. Allow your dog to work independently and balance on you without verbal commands.

If you have tame "knee-knocker" sheep that do not present a challenge, your dog may become bored and want to come past the sheep. Make it a priority to get out in different fields and on different sheep in order to keep your dog interested and challenged.

As with all problems, figuring out the underlying reason(s) for the occurrence will help in formulating the correct solution.

DOG WILL NOT WALK IN TO THE SHEEP

Understanding the reason the dog will not walk in is important. Is he afraid of the sheep? Are the sheep not moving away from the dog? Are the sheep intimidating? Does the dog not understand the command? Is he "sticky" because of being strong-eyed? Understanding the reason behind the problem will help you figure out the correct way to address it.

If your dog is somewhat sensitive, shy or scared of the sheep, be very careful not to work sheep that may be intimidating or that do not stick with you. Be sure you have dog-broke, knee-knocker sheep when starting this type of dog.

Sometimes obedience-trained dogs will be reluctant to break a "Lie Down, Stay" command. Give your release word as a countercommand, followed by the command "Walk In." Make sure you are backing up and have the sheep moving away from the dog as you say "Walk In." This will make your dog think that he is moving the sheep and encourage him to follow them!

If you have a Border Collie that is strong-eyed and is sticky,

Stock dogs must have the desire to work under all conditions of weather and terrain, if they are to be useful in farm work.

causing a resistance walking in, it is important to keep the dog moving, turning and working so that he stays loose and gets used to working sheep while moving. If he does become sticky, slap the crook or turn into him to get him going again.

Later in training, you will *have* to create tough situations in which your dog will really have to push and work to get the sheep to move. *Remember to read your dog! Each dog is an individual* and must be presented with this type of work only when ready for it. Although there are certain tendencies that can be identified within breeds as a group, each breed is made up of individuals that need to be read and worked according to their individual needs.

DOG STOPS SHORT ON THE OUTRUN

There are two main reasons for dogs stopping short on an outrun: (1) You may have a wide-running dog that is up against the fence and feels too close to the sheep to come by them, or (2) a young dog may feel pressure from the sheep wanting to come to you. This causes him to stop short, let the sheep come past and then fall in behind the sheep as they come to you. This is primarily a problem with tame, dog-broke sheep that start to head for the handler the minute the dog is sent on the outrun. This may turn into a bad habit very quickly if allowed to continue.

In order to get your dog to go around, say "Get Out of it," and slap the crook on the ground as he starts to slow down.

This is not always a clear-cut situation, since sometimes your dog may be correct in stopping early! If the dog is reading the pressures correctly and the sheep move straight to you, then you should not get after him for this. This is exactly the kind of independent thinking that you want to see!

Change the placement of the sheep, or change the direction or position from which you are sending your dog relative to the sheep and to pressure points (such as the barn or other sheep). By doing this you may be able to tell if the dog is reading things correctly or if shutting down early has become a bad habit.

In order to describe the correction for the bad habit of stopping short on the Outrun, we'll consider a case in which your dog is stopping short on the Outrun in the "Come Bye" or clockwise direction. As the dog goes out and begins to stop short, run straight out to your left—in the *same direction* as your dog, without moving toward your dog or the sheep. This will place you more out of balance to the dog and encourage him to move on around the sheep. If the dog does not continue around the sheep, then say "Get Out." As a general rule, you should not call the dog back to you; this can quickly become a bad habit. If necessary, shorten the distance of the outrun in order to increase your control over the dog at the top.

DOG OVERRUNS OR SWINGS TOO FAR AROUND AT THE TOP OF THE OUTRUN

It is important that you determine whether your dog is reading the situation correctly and is swinging past the twelve o'clock position because he is reading pressures correctly, or if this has become a bad habit. If he is reading the situation correctly, the sheep will move straight to you on the fetch. If your dog is swinging too far, they will veer off to one side and he will have to swing back to correct the sheep's path.

In order to correct this bad habit, you will run in the direction *opposite* to that in which you have sent your dog when he passes either three or nine o'clock. By the time he gets to twelve o'clock, or the top of the outrun, you will be in a position to help him balance on you and keep him from swinging too far around. This will start your dog thinking about where you are in relation to the sheep and it will teach him to stop at the correct spot.

This problem may be the result of sloppy work because of tame, dog-broke sheep that do not present a challenge. The dog knows the sheep will not be lost and will come right to you, regardless of where *he* is positioned.

DOG CUTS IN AT THE TOP OF THE OUTRUN

Naturally wide-running dogs or talented dogs that are uncomfortable when they come in close will be less inclined to cut in at the top of the outrun than other dogs. Intense dogs may tend to cut in because they would like to come in to the sheep as quickly as possible. But any dog that is continually worked in a narrow field, with sheep that start to move toward the handler before the dog reaches the top of the outrun, will tend to cut in at the top!

To prevent this problem, teach your dog to stay off of the sheep and keep him from cutting in during the initial training. Do the Daisy Wheel Pattern and Sling-Shot Outruns to help the dog widen out (refer back to Diagrams 18 and 19). If your dog is just starting to cut in at the top, make sure your sheep are not leaving before the dog gets out to the top.

It may help to have a friend hold the sheep for you. Be careful when starting this since a young dog may try to balance on and work on the person holding the sheep instead of on you. Make sure the holder stands motionless and does not talk, yell or scare your dog.

If your dog continues to cut in at the top, run out and through the sheep with "calculated anger," surprising the dog and pushing him back away from the sheep.

DOG PASSES SHEEP ON THE FETCH

This is a common problem. It may occur in a dog that has been hard to train. You usually have to be very hard in order to get this kind of dog to pay attention to you. Therefore, the dog may be very attuned to you, looking *past* the sheep and at you instead of at the sheep. Tame, dog-broke sheep that offer no challenge to the dog may contribute to the development of this problem, as does working only small numbers of sheep. One way to help solve this problem is to work different sheep and as many sheep as possible! This will give your dog more to do and concentrate on, so as not to pay so much attention to you.

If while you are working more sheep, your dog goes past or leaves some sheep, let him go 15 to 20 yards beyond them. Then stop the dog and say "Look Back." If he doesn't go back to pick them up, walk past the sheep he is bringing to you so that you are between these sheep and the dog, repeating the dog's name and the "Look Back" command. Keep walking back toward the sheep that have been left until your dog finally spots them. When he realizes these sheep are left and starts toward them, give a directional command to help get the dog around *behind* the sheep. After he has brought all of the sheep to you, set up for another outrun.

Once your dog has learned the "Look Back," *do not* give the flanking direction. Save the flanking directions for when you need to stop and direct him to get sheep missed in the field on the outrun. Use the "Look Back" without a flanking direction when your dog is leaving or passing sheep on the fetch. In this case, you want the dog to go back, pick up his pressure point and bring the sheep he has left, in order to bring them *all* to you. He will start to realize not to leave those sheep! Your dog must be able to figure out on his own which way to go to get the sheep back together.

You will tell your dog, "Get Out of that! Look Back." You can show aggravation in your voice when giving the command "Get Out of that," but *make sure you do not make the "Look Back" sound like a reprimand*.

If you work this way, using large numbers of sheep, your dog should stop passing the sheep on the fetch. Try to let your dog think independently whenever possible. For instance, if you see the dog hesitate when starting to leave some sheep behind, be quiet and don't immediately give a command. See if *he* will figure it out. *If you always tell your dog what to do, he will never be able to think independently and will not be able to handle things when having to work on his own!*

DOG TRIES TO CIRCLE ON THE DRIVE

Almost all Border Collies and most other gathering dogs will try to circle at some point on the drive. They are following their natural instincts to gather. In order to get your dog to stop trying to go around the sheep and to understand that you want him to drive, use a long line. The long line is there only to prevent the dog from going around the sheep. *It should not be held taut or become a restraint* to keep your dog behind the sheep. The dog should feel free to work back and forth behind the sheep.

It is likely that your dog will want to swing around the sheep in his preferred or comfortable direction. Every time you have your dog walk in, if he likes to go in the "Come Bye" direction, he will tend to walk in on your left side. If he likes to go in the "Away to Me" direction, he will tend to walk in on your right side. It is important to practice until you can be on either side while driving.

If he starts to bear off to one side in order to swing around the sheep, say "Here, Here, Walk In, Steady now." If he is trying to go around to the "Away to Me" side, it may help for you to walk over to your dog's left. He may then change and drift slightly to the right (the "Come Bye" direction) to balance on you. Be ready to check him with the long line or step on it in order to keep the dog from going all the way around the sheep. By doing this, your dog will learn to walk on steadily while driving.

If you allow slipping around the sheep to become a habit, you will find that you will not be able to shut your dog down when you need him to flank while driving.

Another thing that may contribute to a dog cheating, that is, swinging around to circle the stock while driving, is allowing your dog to slip around and bring the sheep to you without making a distinct break between the drive and the fetch. *Never allow a young dog to do this!* To make it clear, always have your dog lie down. Then call him off the sheep and bring him back to your feet. Then send him on an outrun to bring the sheep to you.

DOG LOOKS BACK WHILE DRIVING

A lot of dogs continually look back at the handler while driving. This may be the result of a combination of lack of intensity and lack of self-confidence. They may have tried to slip around the sheep a few times and have been called back. They may be worried about whether or not they are doing the right thing. Most dogs will work out of this and become more confident as they become accustomed to driving.

If you have a dog that looks back continually while driving, be sure that you do not use any hand gestures that will attract attention. Also, do not call his name—give the directions for "Walk In," "Lie Down" or "Get Up" without saying the dog's name in front of or between these commands. Allow your dog to drive with as few commands as possible.

It also may help for you to position yourself out to the side of your dog, rather than behind. That position allows him to see you without turning his head and breaking contact with the sheep. This will help instill confidence in driving.

Don't call him back to you. Do not do a lot of flanking. Practice a lot of straight driving or driving around the field in an oval with a minimum of verbal commands. Encouraging your dog to work independently will help increase confidence and should decrease or eliminate the tendency to look back while driving.

DOG LEAVES THE SHEEP AND STRAYS ON THE FETCH OR THE DRIVE

Although sometimes seen in Border Collies, this is primarily a problem in other herding breeds. The dog may leave the sheep and go sniff something. Give a quick reprimand, "Get Out of that." As soon as your dog comes back *to* the sheep, praise him ("That's a good dog").

In breeds other than the Border Collie, this problem may be caused by lack of intensity, but in Border Collies it may be caused by boredom. If the sheep are not a challenge and the dog knows they are always going to come straight to you, he may not see any reason not to sniff or explore more interesting things! I cannot stress enough *the importance of getting your dog onto different sheep, rotating your sheep so that your dog does not always have the same sheep to work and/or taking your sheep to different places.*

If the problem is caused by lack of intensity or other factors, such as bitches in season, respond according to the situation. Encourage a dog that is not intense and praise him for coming back to work. You may have to reprimand the dog that is interested in other things (other dogs, smells) more sharply, and then praise him as he comes back to work.

DOG "WALKS ON" THE HANDLER

If your dog is constantly disobedient and does not obey your commands, he is "walking on you." Early in training you will, of course, be more lenient, but there comes a time when your dog needs to obey you promptly in order to progress in training. It is time to take back your control and establish or re-establish your command over this dog!

Put your long line back on the dog so that you can enforce your commands. As you are walking out to the sheep, have your dog walk slowly and respond to your "Steady, Walk In, Steady" command. Have him lie down every few body lengths while walking in. If he does not lie down or steady up immediately when you ask, give the line a jerk, using the amount of correction necessary to get the job done. It is important to establish your command over instinct as soon as you can.

DOG APPROACHES SHEEP TOO AGGRESSIVELY

If you are just starting a very aggressive dog, be prepared to defend your sheep. Slap your boogie bag or crook on the ground to help intimidate and keep him out and away from the sheep. As your dog gets out to a comfortable distance, he will learn to be comfortable and not to be so aggressive. When you start to wear with him, don't let him get in too close. Teach him to *walk* right behind the sheep. Keep on and be consistent.

If your dog is approaching the sheep too aggressively or too fast at the top of the outrun, you will have to run right through the sheep at him and blow him out and away from the sheep with "calculated anger" (see chapter 6).

DOG IS A POOR TRAVELER

Your dog may be a poor traveler, being rowdy in the car and wanting to "chase" cars, trucks or bikers inside the car, or getting carsick. To prevent these types of problems, it is important frequently to take your dogs in the car as puppies. If you have an older dog that already has these problems, I advocate using a crate. Use a closed crate with solid sides, not a wire crate. If your dog can't see things flashing by, he is less likely to want to chase them or to get carsick.

It is important for the young pup to be socialized early in order to avoid later behavioral problems. Be sure that the future stock dog learns to be comfortable around children and in a variety of situations.

If you have to drive somewhere to work sheep, your dog may learn to anticipate going to work and having fun, and the ride will become easier and more enjoyable.

An alternative for dogs that are rowdy in the car is to tie them into the seat belt attachment or to the frame under the seat on a short lead. Sometimes this mild restraint will discourage them and/or give you a chance to reprimand or correct them should they start to get rowdy.

DOG WOULD RATHER PLAY THAN WORK

This may occur in very laid-back dogs, including Border Collies, or any dog that is used to playing with you with a ball, stick or Frisbee. If your dog is keen to work, he will usually settle down and go to work within two or three days, and will understand the difference between play time and work time. With less enthusiastic or keen dogs, you must gradually encourage them and teach them to keep working.

DOG IS AGGRESSIVE TOWARD OTHER DOGS OR PEOPLE

This can be a tremendous problem if you want to compete in trials or have your dog out in public! If you know your dog may be aggressive to other dogs or people, it is your responsibility to keep a leash or line on him when walking and a crate for when the dog is not active.

This problem may sometimes be prevented by proper socialization and handling of your puppy and young dog. Teaching your dog to walk and stand on a loose leash and not to invade other dog's or people's territory is basic to having a well-behaved dog and basic to common courtesy for other dogs and people. Teach your dog to sit or stand on a loose leash to be petted and to ''meet'' people. Don't allow him to go to other people or dogs uninvited, or to demand attention.

Select carefully if you intend to use your puppy for stock work; the puppy should not be overly fearful of human contact, and should be comfortable when held.

Be careful how you handle your dog while establishing these habits. If you are constantly restraining, pulling back and/or speaking to him with a concerned or anxious tone of voice, he may misinterpret your intentions. He may think you are afraid or anxious about these other dogs or people, and may become *more* aggressive. As recommended for all problems, make sure you give a verbal correction that will be backed up by a physical correction, if necessary. Make sure your correction makes an impression on your dog. Praise and let your dog know when his behavior is appropriate, but don't praise so enthusiastically that you get him excited.

With a very aggressive dog, considerable force may be necessary and you may have to set the stage to meet other dogs or people that are aware of the dog's nature and are knowledgeable about training. Consider staging this at a time and place at which it is appropriate and easy for you to correct your dog. If you are unsure about how or when to do these things, consult a professional trainer or knowledgeable breeder who may be willing to help you.

Be aware that your dog's personality may change as sexual maturity is reached. Both female and male dogs, perhaps especially male dogs, will perceive other dogs and people differently when they become sexually mature, usually between eight and twelve months of age. Puppies that never had a problem with other dogs or people may begin to challenge them and/or resist human authority.

Some aggressive personalities are the result of breeding and cannot be easily overcome, if at all, regardless of your expertise.

DOG CHASES CATS AND OTHER SMALL ANIMALS

Border Collies and other dogs that are intense about herding may be very attracted to cats or small animals, such as rabbits or squirrels, whose movements may encourage the dog to chase or show varying degrees of aggression. Some are satisfied with chasing and/or nipping, while others want to kill their prey. This may be a problem if dogs are allowed to roam off leash and unsupervised. It is easier to prevent this habit by never allowing it to get started than it is to cure it once it is established.

Your herding dog *can* be taught to respect any type of animal and to leave them alone. It will require you to be consistent with your corrections and to anticipate situations in which problems may occur.

It may be more difficult with some dogs than others, but is not impossible to accomplish. Use of a retractable leash may help you get control of a dog that takes off suddenly after cats or other small animals. Be sure you have a leash that will not snap or break when your dog hits the end of it at full speed! Be sure to say "No, Leave It" or whatever command you have chosen just prior to your dog getting to the end of the leash. Proper *timing* of your correction followed by an abrupt stop can be very effective!

DOG CHASES CARS

This problem is similar to the one above—the dog that wants to chase and/or attack cats or other small animals. It is an expression of the instinct to herd moving things, and is a leading cause of death in herding dogs that are allowed to roam freely or that escape from confinement.

Numerous methods exist for breaking dogs from chasing cars. As with most learned behavioral problems, it is best to prevent them in the first place, rather than wait until they are established.

Sometimes dogs that are put into work in a regular training program will lose their desire to chase cars once they have productive work to do and are exercised regularly. Other dogs are inveterate car chasers and may continue to want to chase cars even when they receive plenty of exercise and are in training. For such a dog, severe physical correction coupled with repeated staged events may be necessary to persuade him that what will be received from you is not worth the few seconds of fun chasing that car! When you are not around, it is best to keep your dog confined. This will ensure his safety and your peace of mind!

10

Trialing for Stock Dogs

PURPOSE OF TRIALS

The first unofficial stock dog trials started in Great Britain at least a century ago. These competitions were started, I'm sure, when the shepherds got together in the pubs and started bragging about whose dog could do what best. Pretty soon the bets were on, and they started arranging competitions and practicing for them. These first competitions were set up to involve real farm tasks, since after all the dogs were owned primarily for their daily usefulness; and yet these competitions soon needed a set of consistent guidelines so that dogs could be measured more or less by the same yardstick. Just as is the case today, the purpose of these early trials was to see whose dog was the best, although it's gotten quite competitive now. Originally the trials were between one farmer and another, and now the competitions have progressed to prime time British television!

The key point to remember, when you are training your stock dog, is that *you should never train for a trial*; that's always a mistake. You may want to get your dog ready for a particular trial by setting up specific training situations, but when you begin your training program you should train with the goal not of competing, but of getting the most out of your dog. You want to train so that you could do actual work with your dog, no matter what breed or type of dog you have.

People who train for competition rather than for actual farmwork leave tremendous holes in the dog's training. For example, if you trained only for trials you would never work your dog on a large number of sheep, since trials generally use only four to six sheep at a time. This is an enormous mistake, because when you put the dog on a large number of sheep, you discover that he doesn't have any idea of how to move them and how to hold them together. The only way you can help your dogs to learn the techniques of controlling a large flock is to let them practice on a large flock. Let them learn how large groups of sheep or cattle behave. You must work as many sheep you as can, as often as you can.

There are, of course, times when you *should* work just a few sheep, because dogs who have worked *only* large flocks can get very "pushy" and hard to hold. The important thing to remember is to vary the exercises in your training program so as to finish with a well-rounded, useful, confident dog.

The progressive training program outlined in this book works toward that goal. It includes very little work aimed specifically at getting your dog ready for a trial; rather, the purpose is so that you can get actual work done on the farm or ranch. No matter what breed of herding dog you are working with or how much actual farmwork they will need to do, you will have a better herding dog if you keep that goal in mind, rather than if you train just to compete.

In training your dog, one of the most important guidelines to remember is to bring out as much of the *natural ability* in your dog as you can. You should try to find the optimum balance between the dog working on natural ability and by consistent obedience to your commands. Different breeds, and different dogs within those breeds, have varying degrees of natural ability, which the trainer must be aware of. You should be careful not to put dogs in over their heads.

But often we can get a dog to do more than natural ability would allow, by putting command in front of the instinct. That way, when a dog doesn't instinctively know what to do, at least that dog will do what we say when we say it, which can get both dog and trainer through many potential problems. But the trainer should not overcommand the dog, especially in the early stages of training. It is very important to encourage the dog to think independently as you try to develop that animal's fullest ability as an individual.

Close-contact work, as outlined in chapter 6, is helpful in this process, both for the dog's general usefulness and for competition.

In these photos, the author demonstrates the dog's natural wearing ability, and then pens the sheep using three dogs simultaneously.

Frequently, in a trial situation, the sheep will get up against a fence, even though that is not a planned part of the course; so the dog must feel comfortable pulling the stock off the fence. This type of situation is where the rubber meets the road in a trial; it will show whether you've done your homework properly, whether your dog will react and work properly in high-stress situations when problem solving is a must.

Trials are very high-stress situations both for dogs and their owners; you must have your dog trained to be able to handle those situations, and you must have yourself under control as well. It's very important to psyche yourself up to have the confidence you need to control the situation, and your dog also must have the confidence necessary as well.

BORDER COLLIE TRIALS

Several different organizations sponsor stock dog trials, and each group has its own set of guidelines and classifications. Border Collie trials throughout the United States, for the most part, follow the international set of guidelines outlined by Great Britain's International Sheep Dog Society. Competition is divided into four basic classes: Novice, Pro-Novice, Nursery or Ranch and Open. Each of these classes involves a course which includes some or all of the following tasks, at varying levels of difficulty: Outrun, Lift, Fetch (these three tasks together constitute the Gather), Wear, Drive, Pen and Shed or Split. These terms are defined in chapter 2 of this book.

Novice classes generally include beginning handlers and beginning dogs. The course includes a Gather of about 100 yards, sometimes a Wear (with the dog holding the sheep to the handler), and a Pen. If you have the chance to start out in the Novice class, it's awfully good to let the dog work up to the higher classes gradually. Starting out in the Novice class puts mileage on, gets the dog used to running in trials, and it helps you get used to being out there as well! This preparation can be very beneficial when you get into the Open trials, where you are sometimes dealing with tremendous competition.

The **Pro-Novice** classes are designed for beginning handlers who have bought dogs that have already been running at the Open level, for experienced handlers with beginning dogs, or for Novice dogs and handlers who are ready to move up one level. This class usually will consist of a longer Outrun, Lift and Fetch, and then will involve a

Drive through one or more panels. The full-course Drive is set up like a triangle, with the handler at one corner, and a panel at each of the other corners; the dog would Drive the sheep in a straight line from the handler to one of the panels or gates, then straight across to the other panel (this portion is called the "Crossdrive"), and finally in a straight line back to the handler.

The next step up from the Pro-Novice class is what is generally called the **Ranch class, the Open Ranch class**, or **the Nursery class**. These dogs run a full course, the same course as an Open or advanced class, except generally without the Shed or Split.

The most advanced class of trial competition is the **Open class**, where advanced dogs and professional trainers compete in tremendously stiff competition. For this level of trailing, you need a dog accustomed to working in a lot of different areas, with the right mental attitude when out there, and one that can take a lot of orders over a long period of time. A dog that is tremendously athletic and has the natural ability to think and work independently is a big asset here. At the same time, the Open dog has to do what you ask and not question your authority. Usually Open dogs will not win or place in the top ten consistently until they are at least four or five years old, because they don't settle down and get the mileage they need to put it all together— although there are exceptions.

Throughout the U.S. there are many different associations that have to do with the Border Collie, some specific to a state and some to a geographic region. There is one national association called the United States Border Collie Handler's Association (USBCHA). This association is designed strictly with trials in mind.

OTHER HERDING ORGANIZATIONS

The American Kennel Club is, as far as I know, the largest organization that sets up Trials for breeds other than the Border Collie. This organization has developed a Herding division; the specific rules and regulations for their Herding competitions are being adapted continuously as they attempt to set up competitions suitable for many different breeds, and to maximize the herding instinct in breeds for whom this original function has long been overlooked.

Because of this broader goal, their task is more difficult than that of breed-specific organizations. The AKC, as well as any organization, has to be careful not to get bogged down in rule books, making the rules so technical that they don't leave any room for animal behavior. As the saying goes, it is important that you don't tie your hands behind your back and then try to put up wallpaper. Herding is a relatively new area for the AKC, and as they go through their growing pains, they will continue to draw on the knowledge that they have in order to make it a viable working division.

The American Herding Breed Association (AHBA) and the Australian Shepherd Club of America (ASCA) also hold stock dog trials throughout the United States. Specific rules for the competitions vary among these different organizations, based on the particular talents and abilities of the breeds involved. In general, however, the trials set up by the AKC, AHBA and ASCA involve the same basic tasks as in the Border Collie trial: the Gather, Wear, Drive, Pen and Shed.

Since regulations about distances, time limitations and judging differ so widely, it is advisable to contact the organizations in which you are involved for specific details. However, if your training program is aimed toward producing a well-rounded and useful stock dog, as it should be, then both your dog and you will be able to adjust to these variations and compete in different types of trials.

GENERAL REQUIREMENTS FOR TRIALING

Dog Characteristics

Generally speaking, it takes the same type of dog for beginning level trials as for Open trials. He must have a level of intensity that will help keep him on the field. With breeds other than the Border Collie that level of intensity is harder to find. Some of the other working breeds are highly motivated or have a high level of intensity; many other breeds have had that intensity bred out of them. It is extremely important, as you start to work a young dog, to evaluate the dog's level of intensity. If you intend to do a fair amount of trialing, your dog must have the level of intensity it takes to maintain your training program to the degree required for trialing.

Intensity of work is very important, but the dog also has to enjoy herding, to *want* to stay on the sheep or other stock. The dog must be attuned to the handler. A trial dog cannot be such a hard or dominant dog that will not learn to do what the handler says, and yet cannot be such a sensitive dog that the handler can't make a correction. Without some degree of verbal correction, you will not be able to tune the dog to the degree that you need to get the work done.

Intelligence and inherited ability are essential ingredients as well. The trial dog must have a great deal of inherited ability. As with intensity, this is something that can be very difficult to find, especially in some breeds for generations of which this was not thought to be a desirable or necessary attribute. Many dog clubs, as well as the AKC, today are working toward building back this ability to read stock and to know instinctively what they are doing.

It is very important that the trial dog be able to read stock. However, what isn't there *naturally* may be put in with Obedience commands. The handler must read the stock for the dog, and the dogs must respond and do what is being asked of them. This level of Obedience can cover up a lot of the problems, as long as the dog and you are relatively close to the stock and in a small enough area where you can keep things under control. Having your dog under *control is extremely important* when you are working in a trial, because precision is what it's all about.

Precision and Control

In trialing, as we have discussed, the dog must be working to some degree on a natural ability to read stock and read pressures. However, a dog must have learned "the rules of the game" before going out onto the trial field. This means that, when the dog sees the job that needs to be done, the job must be done *your* way. For example, the dog may feel that gripping the sheep is a very effective tool for moving them, but grips are generally not allowed on the trial field. Some regions are more lenient to grips than others. For example, in the Northeast, sheep are very much accustomed to being worked by dogs, so grips are not necessary. However, many Western trials use range ewes, who just don't take what the dog says as gospel! Sometimes the dog must get a little more severe to make believers out of these sheep, and so grips are more likely to be allowed than they would be in the East.

I have heard many people say (and I have said it myself!), when they come off the trial field with a young dog, "I'll bet if I could try that again I'd get it right." Well, the most difficult part of trialing is that you only get *one try*, and you and the dog have got to be right the first time you get out there. As with all tasks, to achieve this during

The careful training program of your dog will be tested in Trial situations. The dog must be under control and hold the balance point while working at a long distance from the handler.

trialing, you must first have achieved this during training. From the beginning, in your practice sessions, you should teach your dog to make the *first* Outrun a good Outrun. Do not let your dog cheat on you when you are starting your practice session, because that same habit is going to carry through when you get out on the trial field; in fact it will be even worse, because of the added tensions.

Instead, during your training program, set the stage to make that initial Outrun as precise and perfect as you can every time. It's going to fall apart sometimes, that's all there is to it; but when it does, make sure that you correct the dog and straighten things out as quickly as you can so that you can trust the dog the next time. But the less often it falls apart, and the more often the initial Outrun is correct, the better your chances will be on the trial field.

For the AKC, ASCA and AHBA Herding Trials the Outrun is much shorter than it is in the Open trials for the Border Collies, since these associations have geared these trial guidelines to suit to a greater number of breeds, and for a lot of those dogs the longer Outruns are more difficult or even impossible. However, even though the Outrun is much shorter, that does not make it easier; generally you are working in a fenced area that's only about 100 feet by 200 feet, and the dog can't get away from the sheep and enable the sheep to feel relaxed. Because of this closeness, your dog's path on the Outrun in that small area is almost more important than in a bigger area. If the dog doesn't stay off the sheep and hug the fence pretty closely while going up around them, the sheep are going to be very uncomfortable and you are not going to be able to hold things together. So you want to be very careful how you set up and do your initial Outrun and initial work; make sure it's under control at all times. It's a common mistake, at the outset of your practice session, to let your dog run around until tired out and easier to control, but you need that dog under control from the time you walk out onto the field until the time you walk off the field. There's no reason that you can't have that control, with the proper training.

Another important aspect in preparing your dog for trial competition is teaching your dog to take a tremendous number of commands, one right after the other. This is often called screwing the dog down or tightening a dog down. It is very important to practice this type of constant communication when your dog is far enough along in training not to be confused or stressed by this.

To accustom your dog to this, during a training session, work rapid series of commands into the work for 15 or 30 seconds, and then let up for a few minutes. For example as you practice a drive, you generally walk along, letting the dog work the pressures and do his/her own thing, and maybe you are chipping along or telling the dog to walk in. But once in a while, every three or four minutes during the drive, you want to screw the dog right down or tighten right down for 15 or 30 seconds, giving a whistle or voice commands one right after the other: "Way to Me, Stop, Walk In, Stop, Way to Me, Stop, Walk In, Way to Me, Come By, Way to Me, Come Bye, Stop, Walk In," with barely a pause between commands.

In this way you will accustom your dog to take those commands rapidly and without getting frustrated. Often, when you first start practicing this, the dog will get frustrated and fly right in and hit the sheep, because of not being used to taking commands so rapidly. It's just as important to cover those bases with your training as it is with the others. Of course, in a trial, you are probably more excited than you are at home, and so quite possibly the dog is more excited, and the sheep also are probably apprehensive about things, so it's important that your dog understand and react to the many commands you are giving without falling apart. As always, the dog will perform to this level when you ask *only* if you have done your homework, and you have trained the dog specifically to take that kind of command work.

PREPARING YOURSELF AND YOUR DOG FOR COMPETITION

In preparing yourself and your dog for trial competition, it is crucial that you work on different fields and with different sheep if possible, as discussed throughout this book. When you are at home the pressure is always the same, even if you move around on the field, unless you have a very large field or several different types of sheep; but the average handler only has from a half-dozen to a few dozen sheep, and those sheep know that dog pretty well. They probably know each other by name, for goodness sake! That dog knows many things; how the sheep are going to react in every corner of the field, where all the gates are, where all the pressure points are and how to react to them. This can be compared to children who practice solving the same math problems every day; they get tremendously good at those math problems, but when new problems are thrown at them, they do not know how to handle them. If the problems that face this dog every day are the same as the day before, your dog will not learn how to read and react to unexpected situations. So you must get into different circumstances, work with different sheep, and work where the pressures are different.

Some **training exercises** will help your dog learn to read changing pressures while in your own field. One exercise that is very helpful, if you have a big enough flock, is to split off some sheep and work them around the existing flock; practice Wearing, Driving, and short Outruns without letting the 6 to 10 sheep get back to the main flock. This teaches a dog to work pressure, but still will not take the place of going to a new field, with new contours and where the hills and low places are in a different spot, where the gate is in a different spot, or where the sheep are not used to being worked by a dog every day so they might not move off the dog, and the dog has to know how to push. You and your dog just cannot get the education you need by working at home all the time.

As you make plans to compete in a specific trial, it is helpful to

The author is shown here setting up a single dog for Trial competition and setting up two dogs for brace competition.

It is often helpful if trainers use a radio, so that you can hear their instructions and comments while working your dog in the field.

find out what type of sheep the dog will be working with in the trial, and work that same type of sheep, if possible, prior to the trial. For example, if the trial will involve working light and easy-to-move sheep like Barbados sheep, you will want to work them ahead of time to lessen the dog's discomfort because a dog who is accustomed to "heavy," slow-moving sheep will really get keyed up when it is time to hit those *flighty* sheep. Especially if your dog is young or you are just starting to trial, you will not be able to hold the dog in this new situation, and it will be because *you* have not done your homework.

It can be extremely good for you and for your dog to start by competing in **fun matches,** where you have the opportunity and the environment to help or correct your dog a lot more than you would at a real trial situation. When dogs start trialing, they become "trial-wise"; they quickly learn that in a trial you cannot correct them like you can at home, so they will want to do their own thing and do it their own way. But if you enter these fun matches when your dog is still inexperienced, and your dog starts to push you around a little bit, you can correct more. You can work in a more relaxed way, you have the time to correct without getting bounced off the field, and the dog does not ever learn to push you around or make independent decisions on the trial field.

226

As you proceed in trialing, you will become what is called "ring-wise" in the horse world. In some ways trialing is like chess; you have to be thinking two or three moves ahead, enabling you to have your dog placed where needed in order to prevent problems from arising. You have to be defensive in your running. Rather than trying to react always to the sheep's movement, you need to learn to *move the dog before the sheep move* so that they move in the direction *you* want them to go instead of the direction *they* wanted to go. Participating in fun trials gives you time to put this all together, think it through, and practice thinking ahead.

Penning is a difficult task that is required even at the Novice level of trialing. It takes effort to set up a Pen, but it is well worth that effort; penning is a task that involves a great deal of fine tuning for you and for your dog. The dog must understand what you are trying to do, and then must practice precision and control in accomplishing the task. Reading the sheep and their intentions is crucial in penning, for both you and your dog; techniques for getting your dog ready to Pen, and for practicing penning, are discussed in chapter 6.

During trials, and as you review your performance afterward, you, the handler, also have to practice reading the sheep, reading pressure, understanding why your dog reacted in an unexpected way. This too can be practiced during your regular training sessions. As you are out there practicing with your dog, and you see things happening, or not happening as you wanted, understand *why* the sheep reacted the way they did; think it through and figure it out in your own mind. Probably the dog reacted in an unexpected way because the pressure was different than you had read it to be; a lot of the time the dog reads pressure better than you do. **Learn from your mistakes, learn from your dog and learn from the sheep**, in order to prevent unpleasant "surprises" on the trial field.

CONCLUSION

Perhaps the most important thing for you to remember, when you first start trialing, is *not to go out there to win*. Of course it's fine if the win comes along, but the most important thing is to go out there and hold things together, and do the best job you possibly can, and help your dogs do the best job they possibly can. When you see sheep that are a little wild at a trial, you may have a tendency to feel defeated, to think "Oh, I'll never be able to hold these together"; but what you should try to do is think of it as a challenge, and try to think ahead of the situation and *make* it go together, make it work. You should go in with the attitude that you are there to learn as much as you can from the experience, and to help your dog learn as much as possible.

Of course the higher echelons of trialing are more competitive than the lower classes, but the Novice class is definitely supposed to be a learning experience both for the handler and for the dog. If you miss a Fetch gate or a panel, it's no big deal. You don't want to be too lax about it, but if you do miss a panel, ask yourself "why did that happen? What could I have done differently in order to have held that together properly?" Or if you happen to draw a group of sheep with one ewe that is breaking off from the others, think "How can I put this together? should I take the one to the four or the four to the one?" Think it through in your mind so you know more about the stock you are working with and about that particular situation at that particular moment, and learn to think two or three steps ahead.

Take advantage of the opportunity, on the trial field, to evaluate your dog, see where the weaknesses are and where the strong points are, where the dog is able to cope with situations and where the dog is not. After you get off the field, review the experience carefully in your mind so you can figure out what happened, why it happened and all the variables that go into it.

Consider the trial experiences, especially the early ones, as a challenge and an opportunity to find out where the holes or gaps are in your dog or in your training program. It's important to keep all of this in mind when you are working, to make you and your dog better performers in the years to come.

11

In Conclusion

"One cannot be a good teacher without learning and it is difficult to learn without teaching."

J. Willis Hurst, author

RECOGNIZING GOOD INSTRUCTION

Good instruction will take place in a safe environment. An effective training center does not have to be fancy to be safe and functional. The stock should be in good condition and sound.

Instruction may be in the form of private lessons or clinics. Watching others train and having the opportunity to ask questions and receive thoughtful answers about what you are seeing is invaluable! You may be seeing the answers to problems you will be addressing next week or next year, as well as getting help appropriate for your current level of training.

HOW TO FIND A HERDING INSTRUCTOR

A local breed organization may be able to refer you to herding clubs in your area and/or to experienced herding instructors. Many of the best instructors have a background in training and teaching with

Many trainers offer one- or two-day clinics that can help you to begin or to refine your training program. These pictures show the author giving individual instruction at a training clinic.

Border Collies because this breed has traditionally been used for herding. Working with Border Collies will provide a basis for understanding, recognizing and learning about the herding instinct, styles and natural ability in other breeds. If you have another breed, it may be more difficult to find an instructor experienced in working with those herding breeds. It is a good idea to attend area tests and trials and talk to a variety of people about their impressions of and experiences with various instructors.

No book can take the place of experience in the field and direct instruction while learning and performing. But by reading, learning and thinking, you likely will be better prepared to face the challenge of training your dog and/or improving your handling performance. By understanding the bases for herding, possible instinctual reactions, responses to training, important concepts and key exercises, you should be able to get the most out of your practice and instruction. Good instruction will help you be confident in your interpretation of written material and in confirming whether or not you are executing a training program that fits you and your dog.

If in writing this book, I have been able to help you understand an essential concept, provided you with new insights into your dog's behavior and/or your handling or provided you with new information or ways of approaching stock dog training, I have fulfilled an important goal as an author and teacher. By sharing what took me many years to learn, I hope I have helped you learn more rapidly, saved you time, energy and frustration in your training and advanced the ''art and science'' of stock dog training.

"A WORKING DOG"

I've seen the Rocky Mountains
And the Gulf of Mexico,
The California surfers
And palm trees by the row.

I've read the works of Shakespeare
And seen Picasso's paint,
The sounds of concert pianists
And heard the bagpipes quaint.

And all of these have thrilled me,
but not one could compare
With watching herding dogs a-working,
A single or a pair.

There's magic in each movement
That Mozart never had,
And beauty in each turn
That makes my heart feel glad.

There's science in each answer
Of every whistled tone,
That Newton never thought of
Nor ever was he shown.

There's feeling in the handling
That only poets know,
Or men that work with stock dogs
And feel the teamwork grow.

Wherever life may take you
In sunshine or in fog,
You'll never quite forget it
When once you've worked a dog.

Author Unknown